The American Collection:

COLONIAL HOMES

165 Plans With American Style

The American Collection:
COLONIAL HOMES

Published by Hanley Wood
One Thomas Circle, NW, Suite 600
Washington, DC 20005

Distribution Center
29333 Lorie Lane
Wixom, Michigan 48393

Group Vice President, General Manager, Andrew Schultz
Editor-in-Chief, Linda Bellamy
Managing Editor, Jason D. Vaughan
Senior Editor, Nate Ewell
Associate Editor, Simon Hyoun
Senior Plan Merchandiser, Morenci C. Clark
Plan Merchandiser, Nicole Phipps
Proofreader/Copywriter, Dyana Weis
Graphic Artist, Joong Min
Plan Data Team Leader, Ryan Emge
Production Manager, Brenda McClary

Vice President, Retail Sales, Scott Hill
National Sales Manager, Bruce Holmes
Director, Plan Products, Matt Higgins

For direct sales, contact Retail Vision at (800) 381-1288 ext 6053

BIG DESIGNS, INC.
President, Creative Director, Anthony D'Elia
Vice President, Business Manager, Megan D'Elia
Vice President, Design Director, Chris Bonavita
Editorial Director, John Roach
Assistant Editor, Tricia Starkey
Senior Art Director, Stephen Reinfurt
Production Director, David Barbella
Photo Editor, Christine DiVuolo
Graphic Designer, Mary Ellen Mulshine
Graphic Designer, Jacque Young
Graphic Designer, Maureen Waters
Assistant Photo Editor, David Halpin
Assistant Production Manager, Rich Fuentes

PHOTO CREDITS
Front Cover: Design HPK0800011, for details, see page 18. Photos courtesy of William E. Poole Designs, Inc.
Back Cover: Design HPK0800005, for details, see page 12. Photos by Scott Moore, MWS Photography.

10 9 8 7 6 5 4 3 2 1

Printed in the United States of America

Library of Congress Control Number: 2004116169

ISBN: 1-931131-40-6

The American Collection:
COLONIAL
HOMES

110

112

hanley▲wood

ONLINE EXTRA

Passageway

Go to:
www.hanleywoodbooks.com/accolonialhomes
for access to the Hanley Wood Passageway,
your passage to bonus home plans, bonus articles, online ordering, and more!

Features of this site include:
• A dynamic link that lets you search and
  view bonus home plans
• Online-related feature articles
• Built-in tools to save and view your
  favorite home plans
• A dynamic web link that allows you to
  order your home plan online
• Contact details for the Hanley Wood
  Home Plan Hotline
• Free subscriptions for Hanley Wood
  Home Plan e-news

Colonial Style

H ow is it that today, 200 years since they first gained popularity, Colonial home designs still capture the imagination of homeowners and architects building new homes? There's an inherent desire to connect with our past, especially with something as permanent as a new home. Homeowners may look to recreate a home of their childhood, or one their ancestors lived in. And most new homeowners look for a style that will fit in their neighborhood, something Colonial homes do well since they are so prevalent.

All of that plays a role, to be sure. But perhaps the most important reason we're still drawn to this architecture is this: Colonial homes still boast the strong aesthetic appeal they had centuries ago.

As American colonists were building a nation, they were also designing and building a timeless American style of home. It's one whose clean lines and distinctive features were often a product of necessity, but form proved to work hand-in-hand with function.

Like the democracy that those same colonists created, the look of Colonial homes has stood the test of time—even as details in their design have evolved. Specifically, interiors have transformed since the earliest designs, which often featured two rooms on the first floor—the "hall" and "parlor."

The homes you'll find in this book feature historically accurate exteriors, with the distinctive dormers and stately columns that define Cape Cods and Greek Revivals, respectively. But inside you'll find more modern floor plans, designed to fit the lifestyles of today's families.

Gone are the old halls and parlors, or the small, boxy rooms that were popular in the 18th Century because they were easy to keep warm. Instead you'll find open, free-flowing floor plans that connect living spaces together, like kitchens that open gracefully into breakfast areas and great rooms. You'll also find easy transitions between indoors and out, especially with patios and decks in the back of the home.

In these pages you'll find everything from simple saltbox farmhouses to extravagant Greek Revival mansions. Given the geographic expanse of the original colonies, the diversity of the colonists' heritage, and the time frame we consider Colonial—which stretches nearly 200 years—it's not surprising that Colonial homes encompass a wide range of architectural styles.

Each of those styles is represented in the following pages, in gorgeous full color with detailed floor plans. And you can order blueprints for your own piece of American history. ■

Facing page: Approaching a fine Colonial home, like Design HPK0800123 (opposite and page 128), can feel like stepping back in time. This page: Large, welcoming front porches are a hallmark of Southern Colonials like Design HPK0800045 (top and page 48) and Design HPK0800124 (above and page 129).

BOTTOM: CHRIS A. LITTLE FROM ATLANTA, CHATHAM HOME PLANNING, INC.; TOP: PHOTO COURTESY OF: WILLIAM E. POOLE DESIGNS, INC. PHOTO BY COLBERT HOWELL

SOUTHERN
BELLE

The full-height entry, complete with four Ionic columns, dominates the facade of this Early Classical Revival home. This style, popular in the American South from about 1770-1830, was championed by Thomas Jefferson, who used it at Monticello. The symmetrical exterior is highlighted here by the four impressive chimneys, and the curving fanlight above the front door helps distinguish the design from the later Greek Revival period. The front porch is most prominent, but outdoor space is embraced throughout; a veranda features an outdoor kitchen, while the back porch and glorious master suite overlook an ideal spot for a pool and spa.

PHOTO BY: MARK ENGLAND

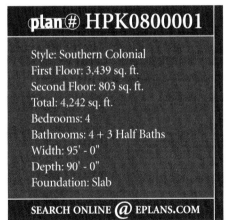

The distinctive impression created from the first look at the exterior of this home (opposite) continues once you step inside. A balcony overlooking the living room also houses a library, with built-in bookshelves included on both ends (left). The living room includes built-ins of its own, plus soaring ceilings that contribute to the impressive feel in the space (above).

plan⊕ HPK0800001

Style: Southern Colonial
First Floor: 3,439 sq. ft.
Second Floor: 803 sq. ft.
Total: 4,242 sq. ft.
Bedrooms: 4
Bathrooms: 4 + 3 Half Baths
Width: 95' - 0"
Depth: 90' - 0"
Foundation: Slab

SEARCH ONLINE @ EPLANS.COM

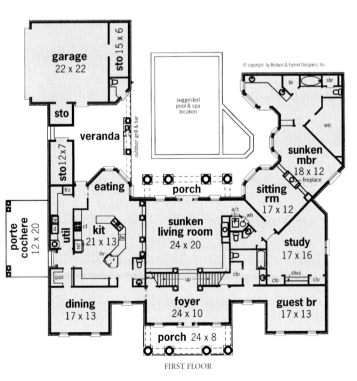

FIRST FLOOR

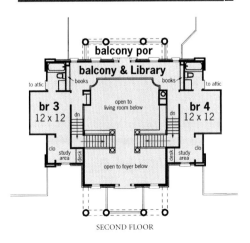

SECOND FLOOR

LONGVIEW

Step back in time and enjoy this graceful home, sitting proudly on a hill. Greek Revival touches like the columned portico lend the home its historic appeal. Inside, the gourmet kitchen, breakfast area, and keeping room are connected by the beamed ceiling, and warmed by one of the three fireplaces on the first floor. A spacious, two-story living room boasts another one, as does the library, which has a private door to the master bedroom. Upstairs, a balcony overlooks the living room, while three more bedrooms each boast a private bath. A rec room offers flexibility, and could be used as a home theater for movie buffs or a play room for children.

PHOTO BY: JEFF S. OTTO

The enchanting facade features curb appeal indicative of the luxury found within (opposite page). The grand foyer features a two-story ceiling and is flanked by the wrapping staircase.

LEFT: PHOTO COURTSEY OF: HICKORY CHAIR FURNITURE. RIGHT: PHOTO COURTSEY OF: WILLAIM E. POOLE DESIGNS, INC. THIS HOME, AS SHOWN IN THE PHOTOGRAPHS, MAY DIFFER FROM THE ACTUAL BLUEPRINTS.

plan# HPK0800002

Style: Greek Revival
First Floor: 3,463 sq. ft.
Second Floor: 1,924 sq. ft.
Total: 5,387 sq. ft.
Bedrooms: 4
Bathrooms: 5½
Width: 88' - 6"
Depth: 98' - 0"
Foundation: Crawlspace, Basement

SEARCH ONLINE @ EPLANS.COM

The open layout enables viewers to admire almost the entire first floor with one glance (above left). The keeping room has the same beam ceiling as in the kitchen and breakfast nook (above right).

3 CAR GARAGE
22'-0" X 36'-0"

© William E. Poole Designs

TRELLIS ABOVE

TERRACE AREA

SINK
UTILITY 1
D. W.

REAR ENTRY   PORCH

MASTER SUITE BEDROOM
19'-0" X 15'-0"

LIVING ROOM
24'-0" X 20'-0"
2 STORY CEILING

KEEPING ROOM
16'-3" X 15'-0"

LINE OF BALCONY ABOVE

VESTIBULE

WARDROBE
WARDROBE

BREAKFAST
11'-8" X 11'-8"

POWDER ROOM

PANTRY

MASTER BATH

MASTER SUITE LIBRARY
15'-6" X 18'-0"

FOYER
15'-0" X 18'-0"
OPEN TO ABOVE

DINING ROOM
15'-6" X 18'-0"

KITCHEN
15'-6" X 14'-0"
FRIG. SINK DW

RANGE

PORTICO   FIRST FLOOR

ROOF AREA

ROOF AREA

COVE CEILING

OPEN TO BELOW

UTILITY 2
DRY
FOLD DN IRON BD

STORAGE
9" CEILING BREAKLINE
OPEN

ROOF AREA

BEDROOM 4
15'-6" X 15'-1"

LINEN

HANDRAIL

REC. ROOM
15'-6" X 29'-0"

LOUNGE
15'-0" X 10'-8"

STORAGE

HANDRAIL

9" CEILING BREAKLINE

STORAGE

BEDROOM 2
15'-6" X 14'-4"

OPEN TO BELOW

DOWN

BEDROOM 3
15'-6" X 12'-8"

PORCH ROOF
WROUGHT IRON RAIL

SECOND FLOOR

EARLY AMERICAN COLONIALS

The first homes in America, particularly in New England, reflected the medieval styles colonists brought with them from Europe. Designs were relatively small and very simple—the Cape Cods and saltboxes of this period had very little ornamentation.

Most homes were two stories, essentially compact boxes with simple, straightforward lines and shingle or clapboard facades. Wood was plentiful and the building material of choice.

The typical side-gabled roof might feature dormers to add space upstairs; some Capes include a long dormer that stretches across most of the rear of the house. Other alterations might include a gambrel roof—which was popular in parts of the Northeast—or a bowed roof often used by Dutch settlers in the mid-Atlantic.

A massive chimney provided warmth, and the rooms were typically small and could be closed off from one another to keep the heat where it was needed.

As families grew, so did their homes. It's common to see older Capes with an ell, or addition, connected to the main part of the house. Often these would link a farmhouse to a barn—a pattern that often continues today in new Capes that connect to garages. ∎

Sharp, clean rooflines decorated with dormers are common on Cape Cod homes like Design HPK0800037 (page 41).

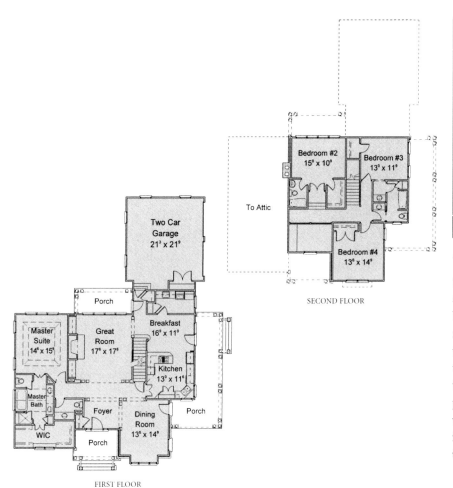

SECOND FLOOR

FIRST FLOOR

plan⊕ HPK0800005

Style: Colonial
First Floor: 1,804 sq. ft.
Second Floor: 1,041 sq. ft.
Total: 2,845 sq. ft.
Bedrooms: 4
Bathrooms: 3½
Width: 57' - 3"
Depth: 71' - 0"
Foundation: Walkout Basement

SEARCH ONLINE @ EPLANS.COM

There's a feeling of old Charleston in this stately home—particularly on the quiet side porch that wraps around the kitchen and breakfast room. The interior of this home revolves around a spacious great room with a welcoming fireplace. The left wing is dedicated to the master suite, which boasts wide views of the rear property. A corner kitchen easily serves planned events in the formal dining room, as well as family meals in the breakfast area. Three family bedrooms, one with a private bath and the others sharing a bath, are tucked upstairs.

ORDER BLUEPRINTS 24 HOURS, 7 DAYS A WEEK, AT 1-800-521-6797

plan# HPK0800006

Style: Colonial
First Floor: 2,814 sq. ft.
Second Floor: 1,231 sq. ft.
Total: 4,045 sq. ft.
Bedrooms: 5
Bathrooms: 3½
Width: 98' - 0"
Depth: 45' - 10"
Foundation: Slab, Basement

SEARCH ONLINE @ EPLANS.COM

This very formal Georgian home was designed to be admired, but also to be lived in. It features handsome formal areas in a living room and formal dining room, but also an oversized family room with a focal fireplace. The master suite sits on the first floor, as is popluar with most homeowners today. Besides its wealth of amenities, it is located near a cozy study. Don't miss the private patio and sitting area with glass in the master bedroom. Upstairs, there are four family bedrooms with great closet space. A three-car garage contains space for a golf cart and a work bench.

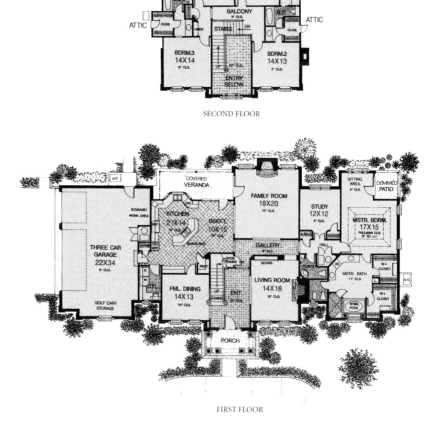

SECOND FLOOR

FIRST FLOOR

SECOND FLOOR

plan # HPK0800007

Style: Colonial
First Floor: 1,809 sq. ft.
Second Floor: 785 sq. ft.
Total: 2,594 sq. ft.
Bonus Space: 353 sq. ft.
Bedrooms: 5
Bathrooms: 4
Width: 72' - 7"
Depth: 51' - 5"
Foundation: Crawlspace, Basement

SEARCH ONLINE @ EPLANS.COM

FIRST FLOOR

With elements of country style, this unique Colonial-inspired home presents a rustic attitude blended with the delicate features that make this design one of a kind. Upon entry, a second-story arched window lights the foyer. Straight ahead, the family room soars with a two-story vault balanced by a cozy fireplace. A pass-through from the island kitchen keeps conversation going as the family chef whips up delectable feasts for the formal dining room or bayed breakfast nook. A bedroom at the rear provides plenty of privacy for guests, or as a home office. The master suite takes up the entire right wing, hosting a bayed sitting area and marvelous vaulted bath. Upstairs, three bedrooms access a versatile bonus room, limited only by your imagination.

plan# HPK0800008

Style: Colonial
First Floor: 1,888 sq. ft.
Second Floor: 1,374 sq. ft.
Total: 3,262 sq. ft.
Bonus Space: 299 sq. ft.
Bedrooms: 3
Bathrooms: 3
Width: 63' - 0"
Depth: 49' - 0"
Foundation: Walkout Basement

SEARCH ONLINE @ EPLANS.COM

This Colonial home speaks of a graceful era. A formal living room with bay window and fireplace joins the dining room with stately columns. The gourmet kitchen has a uniquely angled countertop and a breakfast area. The two-story great room is appointed with a fireplace, a media corner, and a rear staircase. Upstairs, tray ceilings adorn the owners suite's bedroom and bath. Two additional bedrooms and a full bath complete the sleeping quarters.

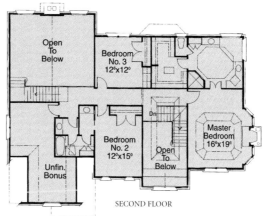

SECOND FLOOR

FIRST FLOOR

SECOND FLOOR

FIRST FLOOR

Quote One®

This charming exterior conceals a perfect family plan. The formal dining and living rooms reside on either side of the foyer. At the rear of the home is a family room with a fireplace and access to a deck and veranda. The modern kitchen features a sunlit breakfast area. The second floor provides four bedrooms, one of which may be finished at a later date and used as a guest suite. Note the extra storage space in the two-car garage.

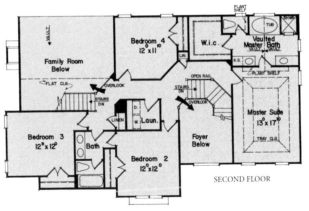

SECOND FLOOR

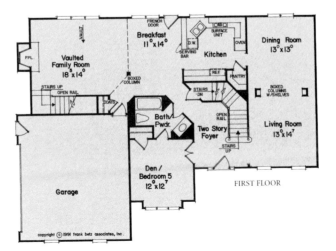

FIRST FLOOR

plan # HPK0800010

First Floor: 1,424 sq. ft.
Second Floor: 1,256 sq. ft.
Total: 2,680 sq. ft.
Bedrooms: 4
Bathrooms: 3
Width: 57' - 0"
Depth: 41' - 0"
Foundation: Crawlspace,
Slab, Basement

SEARCH ONLINE @ EPLANS.COM

A grand two-story foyer takes its charm from a bright clerestory window. Just off the foyer lies the formal living area, where the living room joins the dining room with twin boxed columns that are personalized with shelves. The kitchen is placed to easily serve the dining room, yet it remains open to the breakfast area and vaulted family room. Upstairs, the master suite and bath are nicely balanced with three family bedrooms, a full hall bath, and convenient laundry room.

SECOND FLOOR

FIRST FLOOR

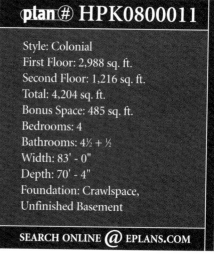

plan# HPK0800011

Style: Colonial
First Floor: 2,988 sq. ft.
Second Floor: 1,216 sq. ft.
Total: 4,204 sq. ft.
Bonus Space: 485 sq. ft.
Bedrooms: 4
Bathrooms: 4½ + ½
Width: 83' - 0"
Depth: 70' - 4"
Foundation: Crawlspace,
Unfinished Basement

SEARCH ONLINE @ EPLANS.COM

Palladian windows, fluted pilasters, and a pedimented entry give this home a distinctly Colonial flavor. Inside, the two-story foyer is flanked by the formal dining and living rooms. The spacious, two-story family room features a fireplace, built-ins, and backyard access. A large country kitchen provides a work island, walk-in pantry, planning desk, and break-fast area. The lavish master suite offers a tremendous amount of closet space, as well as a pampering bath. A nearby study could also serve as a nursery. Upstairs, three bedrooms, each with a private bath, have access to the future recreation room over the garage.

SECOND FLOOR

plan# HPK0800012

Style: Colonial
First Floor: 1,135 sq. ft.
Second Floor: 917 sq. ft.
Total: 2,052 sq. ft.
Bonus Space: 216 sq. ft.
Bedrooms: 4
Bathrooms: 3
Width: 52' - 4"
Depth: 37' - 6"
Foundation: Slab,
Crawlspace, Basement

SEARCH ONLINE @ EPLANS.COM

This grand two-story home proves that tried-and-true traditional style is still the best! Thoughtful planning brings formal living areas to the forefront and places open, casual living areas to the rear of the plan. Bedroom 4 serves as a multipurpose room, providing the flexibility desired by today's homeowner. The second floor is devoted to the relaxing master suite, two secondary bedrooms, a full hall bath, and a balcony overlook.

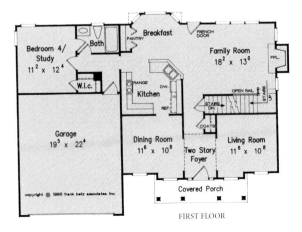

FIRST FLOOR

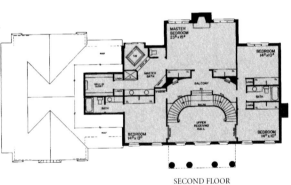

SECOND FLOOR

QUOTE ONE®

plan# HPK0800013

L D

Style: Colonial
First Floor: 2,348 sq. ft.
Second Floor: 1,872 sq. ft.
Total: 4,220 sq. ft.
Bedrooms: 4
Bathrooms: 3½ + ½
Width: 90' - 4"
Depth: 44' - 8"
Foundation: Basement

SEARCH ONLINE @ EPLANS.COM

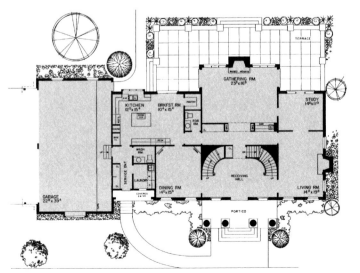

FIRST FLOOR

This classic Georgian design contains a variety of features that make it outstanding: a pediment gable with cornice work and dentils, beautifully proportioned columns, and a distinct window treatment. Inside the foyer, a stunning curved staircase introduces you to this Southern-style home. The first floor contains some special appointments: a fireplace in the living room and another fireplace and a wet bar in the gathering room. A study is offered towards the rear of the plan for convenient home office use. A gourmet island kitchen is open to a breakfast room with a pantry. Upstairs, an extension over the garage allows for a huge walk-in closet in the master suite and a full bath in one of the family bedrooms.

PHOTO BY ANDY LAUTMAN, LAUTMAN PHOTOGRAPHY

20 *The American Collection:* COLONIAL HOMES

ORDER BLUEPRINTS 24 HOURS, 7 DAYS A WEEK, AT 1-800-521-6797

plan ⊕ HPK0800014

Style: Colonial
First Floor: 4,107 sq. ft.
Second Floor: 1,175 sq. ft.
Total: 5,282 sq. ft.
Bonus Space: 745 sq. ft.
Bedrooms: 4
Bathrooms: 4½
Width: 90' - 0"
Depth: 63' - 0"
Foundation: Basement

SEARCH ONLINE @ EPLANS.COM

A sweeping central staircase is just one of the impressive features of this lovely estate home. Four fireplaces—in the library, family room, grand room, and master-suite sitting room—add a warm glow to the interior; the master suite, grand room, and family room all open to outdoor terrace space. There's plenty of room for family and guests—a guest suite sits to the front of the plan, joining the master suite and two more family bedrooms. Upstairs, a large bonus area—possibly a mother-in-law suite—offers a petite kitchen and walk-in closet; a full bath is nearby.

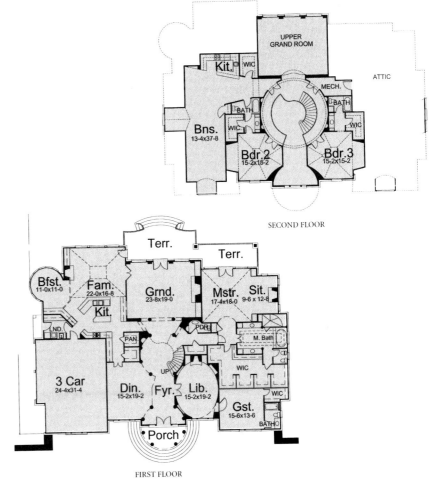

SECOND FLOOR

FIRST FLOOR

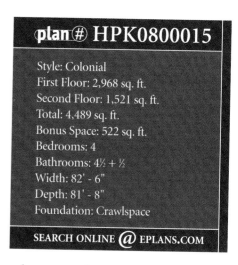

plan # HPK0800015

Style: Colonial
First Floor: 2,968 sq. ft.
Second Floor: 1,521 sq. ft.
Total: 4,489 sq. ft.
Bonus Space: 522 sq. ft.
Bedrooms: 4
Bathrooms: 4½ + ½
Width: 82' - 6"
Depth: 81' - 8"
Foundation: Crawlspace

SEARCH ONLINE @ EPLANS.COM

This home—showcasing elegant Georgian architecture—is reminiscent of the grand homes in the battery section of Charleston, South Carolina. The entry opens to the foyer with its grand staircase. To the right is the hearth-warmed library and to the left, the formal dining room. The foyer leads to the family room where a window wall looks out to the covered porch. A central hall passes the study and proceeds to the luxurious master suite, featuring a windowed tub and a huge walk-in closet. The left wing holds the sunny breakfast area, island kitchen, spacious mudroom, and garage. Upstairs, three bedrooms enjoy private baths and ample closet space.

ORDER BLUEPRINTS 24 HOURS, 7 DAYS A WEEK, AT 1-800-521-6797

This Early American classic was built with attention to the needs of an active family. The formal entrance allows guests to come and go in splendor, and family members can kick off their shoes in the mudroom. The step-saving kitchen is accented by an island for dinner preparations or school projects, and a pantry with tons of space. In the master suite, homeowners can relax in the whirlpool tub and revel in the ample walk-in closet. Second-floor family bedrooms provide privacy, walk-in closets, and two shared baths, both with dual vanities.

SECOND FLOOR

FIRST FLOOR

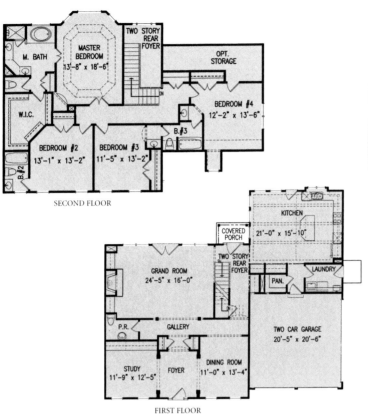

SECOND FLOOR

M. BATH

MASTER BEDROOM
13'-8" x 18'-6"

TWO STORY REAR FOYER

OPT. STORAGE

BEDROOM #4
12'-2" x 13'-6"

W.I.C.

BEDROOM #2
13'-1" x 13'-2"

BEDROOM #3
11'-5" x 13'-2"

B.#3

B.#2

KITCHEN
21'-0" x 15'-10"

COVERED PORCH

GRAND ROOM
24'-5" x 16'-0"

TWO STORY REAR FOYER

LAUNDRY

PAN.

P.R.

GALLERY

TWO CAR GARAGE
20'-5" x 20'-6"

STUDY
11'-9" x 12'-5"

FOYER

DINING ROOM
11'-0" x 13'-4"

FIRST FLOOR

plan# HPK0800017

Style: Early American Colonial
First Floor: 1,602 sq. ft.
Second Floor: 1,334 sq. ft.
Total: 2,936 sq. ft.
Bedrooms: 4
Bathrooms: 3½
Width: 54' - 0"
Depth: 45' - 8"
Foundation: Basement

SEARCH ONLINE @ EPLANS.COM

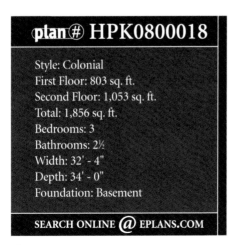

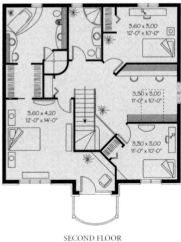

3,60 x 3,00
12'-0" x 10'-0"

3,30 x 3,00
11'-0" x 10'-0"

3,60 x 4,20
12'-0" x 14'-0"

3,30 x 3,00
11'-0" x 10'-0"

SECOND FLOOR

plan# HPK0800018

Style: Colonial
First Floor: 803 sq. ft.
Second Floor: 1,053 sq. ft.
Total: 1,856 sq. ft.
Bedrooms: 3
Bathrooms: 2½
Width: 32' - 4"
Depth: 34' - 0"
Foundation: Basement

SEARCH ONLINE @ EPLANS.COM

4,20 x 3,10
14'-0" x 10'-4"

3,30 x 3,30
11'-0" x 11'-0"

3,50 x 5,80
11'-8" x 19'-4"

4,50 x 5,80
15'-0" x 19'-4"

FIRST FLOOR

plan # HPK0800019

Style: Colonial
First Floor: 1,000 sq. ft.
Second Floor: 1,345 sq. ft.
Total: 2,345 sq. ft.
Bedrooms: 4
Bathrooms: 3½
Width: 57' - 4"
Depth: 30' - 0"

SEARCH ONLINE @ EPLANS.COM

An arched entry, shutters, and a brick facade highlight the exterior of this two-story modern Colonial home. Living and dining rooms at the front of the plan accommodate formal occasions. The rear of the plan is designed for informal gatherings, such as the generous family room, which includes a warming fireplace and bayed conversation area. The bright breakfast area is open to an efficient U-shaped kitchen with a snack bar. Bright windows and French doors add appeal to the living room. Upstairs, a U-shaped balcony hall overlooks the entry below and connects four bedrooms, including a master suite. This retreat features a private sitting room, two walk-in closets, a compartmented bath, separate vanities, and a window-brightened whirlpool tub.

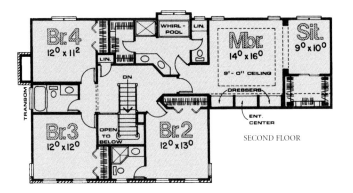

SECOND FLOOR

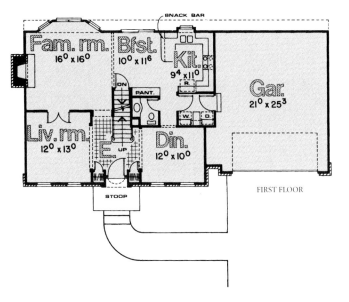

FIRST FLOOR

The pleasing character of this house does not stop behind its facade. The foyer opens to a great room with a fireplace and also to the eat-in kitchen. Stairs lead from the great room to the second floor, where a laundry room is conveniently placed near the bedrooms. The master suite spares none of the amenities: a full bath with a double vanity, shower, tub, and walk-in closet. Bedrooms 2 and 3 share a full bath.

plan# HPK0800020

Style: Colonial
First Floor: 830 sq. ft.
Second Floor: 1,060 sq. ft.
Total: 1,890 sq. ft.
Bedrooms: 3
Bathrooms: 2½
Width: 41' - 0"
Depth: 40' - 6"
Foundation: Walkout Basement

SEARCH ONLINE @ EPLANS.COM

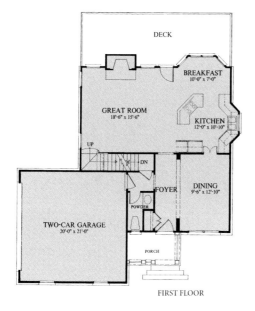

FIRST FLOOR

SECOND FLOOR

Grand, welcoming, and cozy— these are the words that describe this two-story brick house. The first floor consists of a family room with an 18-foot ceiling, a dramatic breakfast nook, a deck, and a guest bedroom with a full bath. Family sleeping quarters are located upstairs. Here you'll find a glorious master suite; it includes His and Hers walk-in closets and a bath with a spa tub, shower, and double-bowl vanity. Bedrooms 3 and 4 share a full compartmented bath. The home is completed with a two-car garage.

SECOND FLOOR

FIRST FLOOR

FIRST FLOOR

SECOND FLOOR

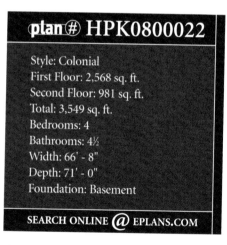

plan# HPK0800022

Style: Colonial
First Floor: 2,568 sq. ft.
Second Floor: 981 sq. ft.
Total: 3,549 sq. ft.
Bedrooms: 4
Bathrooms: 4½
Width: 66' - 8"
Depth: 71' - 0"
Foundation: Basement

SEARCH ONLINE @ EPLANS.COM

A smattering of architectual styles blend effortlessly to create this delightful two-story home. The foyer is flanked by the formal dining room and the living room. To the rear, the island kitchen and breakfast area enjoy a beamed ceiling, bringing a bit of the rustic exterior inside. The family room offers a cozy space for informal gatherings with its warming fireplace. The master suite sits on the far right; Bedroom 2, on the far left, would double easily as a guest room, giving adequate privacy. Two additional bedrooms, each with a private bath, reside on the second floor, as does space for a future rec room.

ORDER BLUEPRINTS 24 HOURS, 7 DAYS A WEEK, AT 1-800-521-6797

SECOND FLOOR

FIRST FLOOR

plan # HPK0800023

Style: Colonial
First Floor: 1,960 sq. ft.
Second Floor: 905 sq. ft.
Total: 2,865 sq. ft.
Bonus Space: 297 sq. ft.
Bedrooms: 4
Bathrooms: 3½
Width: 61' - 0"
Depth: 70' - 6"
Foundation: Walkout Basement

SEARCH ONLINE @ EPLANS.COM

QUOTE ONE®

QUOTE ONE®

SECOND FLOOR

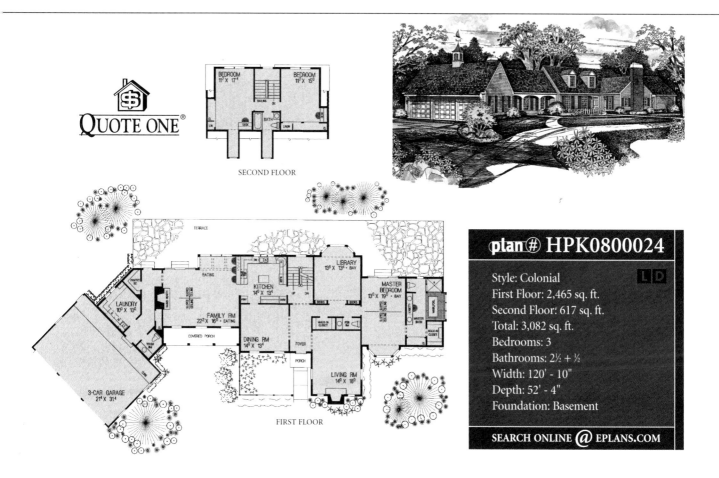

FIRST FLOOR

plan # HPK0800024

Style: Colonial
First Floor: 2,465 sq. ft.
Second Floor: 617 sq. ft.
Total: 3,082 sq. ft.
Bedrooms: 3
Bathrooms: 2½ + ½
Width: 120' - 10"
Depth: 52' - 4"
Foundation: Basement

SEARCH ONLINE @ EPLANS.COM

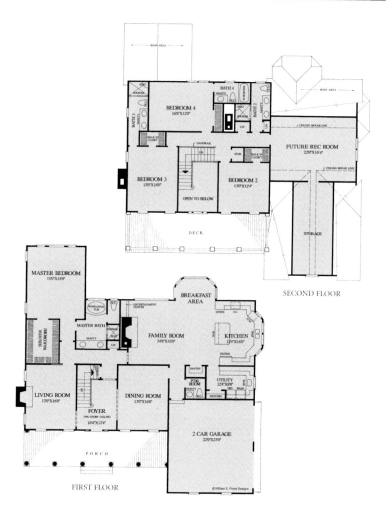

FIRST FLOOR

SECOND FLOOR

plan# HPK0800025

Style: Colonial
First Floor: 2,086 sq. ft.
Second Floor: 1,094 sq. ft.
Total: 3,180 sq. ft.
Bonus Space: 372 sq. ft.
Bedrooms: 4
Bathrooms: 4½
Width: 64' - 4"
Depth: 61' - 10"
Foundation: Crawlspace, Basement

SEARCH ONLINE @ EPLANS.COM

Take one look at this Colonial

haven and you will call it home. A columned front porch and an upstairs deck were built for lazy summer days; the extended-hearth fireplace will warm your heart on chilly winter nights. The living room—with fireplace—and formal dining room are perfect for entertaining. In the bumped-out kitchen and bayed breakfast area, natural light will be the order of the day. The first-floor master suite includes an enormous walk-in closet and a private bath. Upstairs, three generous bedrooms, three baths, and space for expansion will please everyone.

plan # HPK0800026

Style: Colonial
First Floor: 1,992 sq. ft.
Second Floor: 1,458 sq. ft.
Total: 3,450 sq. ft.
Bonus Space: 380 sq. ft.
Bedrooms: 5
Bathrooms: 3½
Width: 108' - 0"
Depth: 64' - 0"
Foundation: Basement

SEARCH ONLINE @ EPLANS.COM

The origin of this house dates back to 1787 and George Washington's stately Mount Vernon. The unusual design features curved galleries leading to matching wings. In the main house, the living and dining rooms provide a large open area, with access to the rear porch for additional entertaining possibilities. A keeping room features a pass-through to the kitchen and a fireplace with a built-in wood box. Four bedrooms, including a master suite with a fireplace, are found upstairs. One wing contains separate guest quarters with a full bath, a lounge area, and an upstairs studio, which features a spiral staircase and a loft area. On the other side of the house, the second floor over the garage can be used for storage or as a hobby room.

QUOTE ONE®

OPTIONAL LAYOUT

OPTIONAL LAYOUT

FIRST FLOOR

SECOND FLOOR

FIRST FLOOR

SECOND FLOOR

BASEMENT

plan# HPK0800027

Style: Colonial
First Floor: 1,376 sq. ft.
Second Floor: 695 sq. ft.
Total: 2,071 sq. ft.
Bedrooms: 3
Bathrooms: 2½
Width: 47' - 0"
Depth: 49' - 8"
Foundation: Basement

SEARCH ONLINE @ EPLANS.COM

The unique charm of this farmhouse begins with a flight of steps and a welcoming, covered front porch. Just inside, the foyer leads to the formal dining room on the left—with easy access to the kitchen—and straight ahead to the great room. Here, a warming fireplace and built-in entertainment center are balanced by access to the rear screened porch. The first-floor master suite provides plenty of privacy; upstairs, two family bedrooms share a full bath. The lower level offers space for a fourth bedroom, a recreation room, and a garage.

plan# HPK0800028

Style: Colonial
First Floor: 1,995 sq. ft.
Second Floor: 1,062 sq. ft.
Total: 3,057 sq. ft.
Bonus Space: 459 sq. ft.
Bedrooms: 4
Bathrooms: 3½
Width: 71' - 0"
Depth: 57' - 4"
Foundation: Basement

SEARCH ONLINE @ EPLANS.COM

Wood siding, muntin window dormers, and a double-decker porch exemplify Southern country style in this welcoming plan. Slide off your porch swing and enter through the foyer, flanked by the bayed living room and dining room. The family room flows effortlessly into the breakfast area and the kitchen, complete with an island. The master bedroom wows with a closet designed for a true clotheshorse. Three upstairs bedrooms enjoy access to the upper porch and space for a future recreation room.

SECOND FLOOR

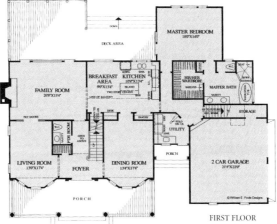

FIRST FLOOR

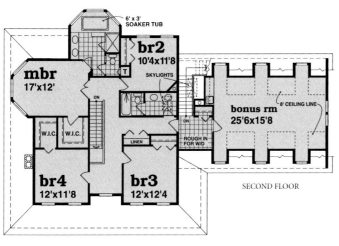

6' x 3'
SOAKER TUB

br2
10'4x11'8

SKYLIGHTS

mbr
17'x12'

DN

bonus rm
25'6x15'8

8' CEILING LINE

W.I.C | W.I.C

LINEN

ROUGH IN
FOR W/D

DN

br4
12'11'8

br3
12'x12'4

SECOND FLOOR

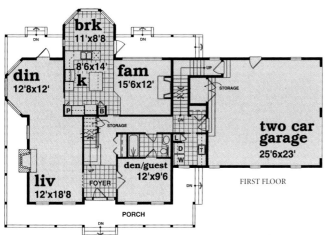

DN

brk
11'x8'8

DN

8'6x14'

UP

din
12'8x12'

k

fam
15'6x12'

STORAGE

P | B

STORAGE

DN

two car garage
25'6x23'

den/guest
12'x9'6

liv
12'x18'8

UP

FOYER

L
D
W

DN

FIRST FLOOR

PORCH

DN

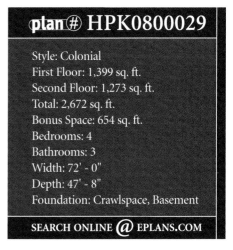

plan# HPK0800029

Style: Colonial
First Floor: 1,399 sq. ft.
Second Floor: 1,273 sq. ft.
Total: 2,672 sq. ft.
Bonus Space: 654 sq. ft.
Bedrooms: 4
Bathrooms: 3
Width: 72' - 0"
Depth: 47' - 8"
Foundation: Crawlspace, Basement

SEARCH ONLINE @ EPLANS.COM

Well proportioned and stunning in stucco, this design is as easy and affordable to build as it is appealing. A sweeping staircase in the two-story foyer leads up to three bedrooms on the second floor. The master suite has a balcony and a full bath with double vanities; each family bedroom has its own bath. The main level includes formal living and dining areas and a family room with deck access. The U-shaped kitchen connects directly to a bayed breakfast nook. A two-car garage joins the house through a service entrance at the mud-room/laundry area.

plan⊕# HPK0800030

Style: Colonial
First Floor: 1,601 sq. ft.
Second Floor: 667 sq. ft.
Total: 2,268 sq. ft.
Bonus Space: 378 sq. ft.
Bedrooms: 3
Bathrooms: 2½
Width: 83' - 4"
Depth: 39' - 8"
Foundation: Crawlspace, Basement

SEARCH ONLINE @ EPLANS.COM

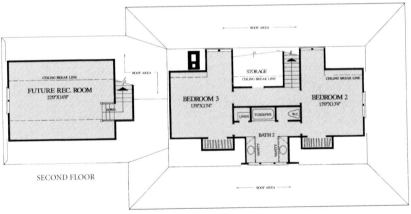

SECOND FLOOR

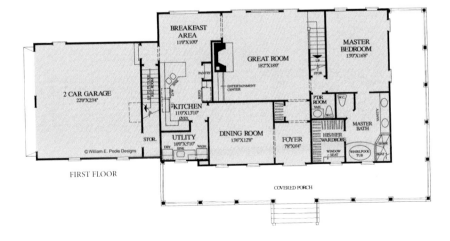

FIRST FLOOR

A welcoming wraparound porch is inviting, with all the charm of a true country cottage. The great room will be the heart of the home; an enchanting extended-hearth fireplace and convenient built-in entertainment center will draw them in—sliding glass doors to the rear property will usher them out. The sunny breakfast area flows into the kitchen and effortlessly continues to the formal dining room. The master suite includes a lavish bath with a whirlpool tub and a generous walk-in closet. Two upstairs bedrooms share a full bath. Future space on the second floor is ready for your imagination.

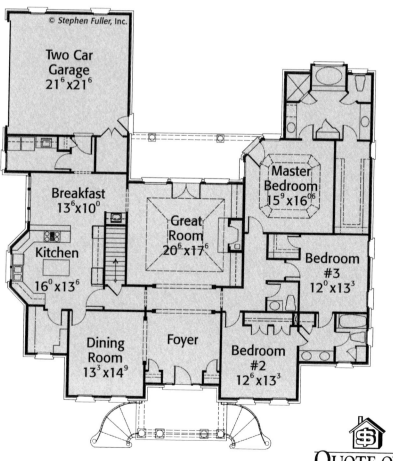

© Stephen Fuller, Inc.

Two Car Garage
21⁶x21⁶

Breakfast
13⁶x10⁰

Kitchen
16⁰x13⁶

Great Room
20⁶x17⁶

Master Bedroom
15⁹x16⁰⁶

Bedroom #3
12⁰x13³

Dining Room
13³x14⁹

Foyer

Bedroom #2
12⁶x13³

plan# HPK0800031

Style: Colonial
Square Footage: 2,697
Bedrooms: 3
Bathrooms: 2½
Width: 65' - 3"
Depth: 67' - 3"
Foundation: Walkout Basement

SEARCH ONLINE @ EPLANS.COM

Dual chimneys (one a false chimney created to enhance the aesthetic effect) and a double stairway to the covered entry of this home create a balanced architectural statement. The sunlit foyer leads straight into the spacious great room, where French doors provide a generous view of the covered veranda in back. The great room features a tray ceiling and a fireplace, bordered by twin bookcases. Another great view is offered from the spacious kitchen with a breakfast bar and a roomy work island. The master suite provides a large, balanced bath and a spacious closet.

QUOTE ONE®

ORDER BLUEPRINTS 24 HOURS, 7 DAYS A WEEK, AT 1-800-521-6797

plan # HPK0800032

Style: Colonial
Square Footage: 1,997
Bedrooms: 4
Bathrooms: 2½
Width: 56' - 4"
Depth: 67' - 4"
Foundation: Crawlspace,
Slab, Basement

SEARCH ONLINE @ EPLANS.COM

Storage
17-4x5-8

Garage
20-4x21-4

Master
Bedroom
12-0x17-1

Bath

Porch
17-4x10-0

1/2
Bath

Laundry
7-4x6-3

Bedroom
11-4x10-0

Bath

Greatroom
17-4x17-4

Pantry

Kitchen/
Breakfast
11-4x20-5

Bedroom
11-4x11-4

Bedroom
11-3x10-1

Foyer

Dining
11-3x13-4

©Larry James Designs

Porch
31-0x8-0

FIRST FLOOR

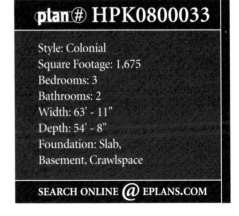

Bath

Master
Bedroom
13-4x12-6

Porch
14-3x10-8

Laundry
9-0x7-5

Kitchen
13-4x11-5

Storage
18-11x7-4

Garage
21-6x21-4

Bedroom
13-3x9-4

Bath

Dining
15-11x9-4

Bedroom
13-4x11-11

Foyer

Greatroom
13-5x15-11

©Larry James Designs

FIRST FLOOR

Porch
34-5x6-0

plan # HPK0800033

Style: Colonial
Square Footage: 1,675
Bedrooms: 3
Bathrooms: 2
Width: 63' - 11"
Depth: 54' - 8"
Foundation: Slab,
Basement, Crawlspace

SEARCH ONLINE @ EPLANS.COM

© Copyright 2004, Garrell Associates, Inc.

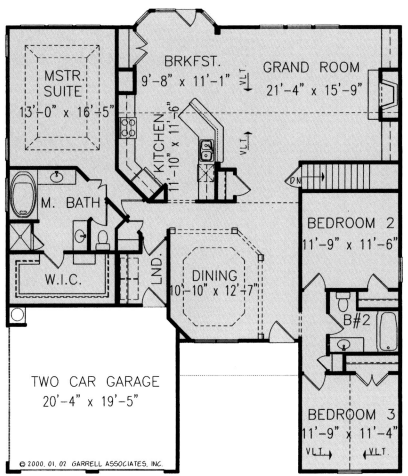

MSTR. SUITE
13'-0" x 16'-5"

BRKFST.
9'-8" x 11'-1"

GRAND ROOM
21'-4" x 15'-9"

V.L.T.

KITCHEN
11'-10" x 11'-6"

V.L.T.

M. BATH

DN

BEDROOM 2
11'-9" x 11'-6"

W.I.C.

LND.

DINING
10'-10" x 12'-7"

B#2

TWO CAR GARAGE
20'-4" x 19'-5"

BEDROOM 3
11'-9" x 11'-4"

V.L.T.   V.L.T.

© 2000, 01, 02 GARRELL ASSOCIATES, INC.

plan# HPK0800034

Style: Colonial
Square Footage: 1,923
Bedrooms: 3
Bathrooms: 2
Width: 48' - 0"
Depth: 53' - 0"
Foundation: Basement

SEARCH ONLINE @ EPLANS.COM

Brick with a hint of siding, keystone lintels, and window shutters complement this home's exterior. To the right of the foyer, find two family bedrooms and a hall bath. To the left, the dining room features a decorative ceiling and defining columns. The grand room, with built-ins and a fireplace, shares a breakfast space and the open kitchen. A private hall leads to the master suite. Full bath amenities and a walk-in closet complete this space.

Christine Cunova 8/02

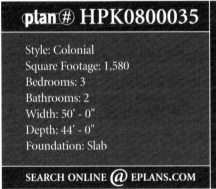

plan# HPK0800035

Style: Colonial
Square Footage: 1,580
Bedrooms: 3
Bathrooms: 2
Width: 50' - 0"
Depth: 44' - 0"
Foundation: Slab

SEARCH ONLINE @ EPLANS.COM

Super-efficient layout combined with attractive exterior elements make this an outstanding starter home. The galley-style kitchen pairs with a breakfast area that is large enough for several people to comfortably keep the cook company. Two family bedrooms flank the dining room. The master suite is buffered by the grand room and offers twin walk-in closets and a private full bath.

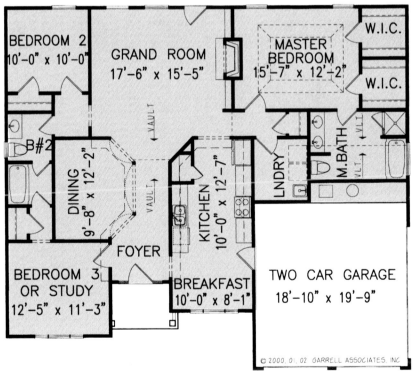

BEDROOM 2
10'-0" x 10'-0"

GRAND ROOM
17'-6" x 15'-5"

MASTER BEDROOM
15'-7" x 12'-2"

W.I.C.

W.I.C.

B#2

DINING
9'-8" x 12'-2"

VAULT

LNDRY

M.BATH

FOYER

KITCHEN
10'-0" x 12'-7"

BEDROOM 3 OR STUDY
12'-5" x 11'-3"

BREAKFAST
10'-0" x 8'-1"

TWO CAR GARAGE
18'-10" x 19'-9"

© 2000, 01, 02 GARRELL ASSOCIATES, INC.

This traditional Cape Cod cottage is a true delight, even if you're not seaside! The enchantment begins with the hearth-warmed great room just off the foyer. It enjoys a wood-beam ceiling and access to the rear porch. A short passageway leads to the comfortable master suite on the right, featuring a twin-vanity bath. At the left of the plan, a formal dining room resides at the front, behind which the island kitchen flows easily into the breakfast area. Pantry space, a half-bath, and a spacious laundry room provide convenience here, as well as access to the two-car garage. Two more bedrooms await on the second floor, sharing a full bath and a hallway to expandable future space.

plan# HPK0800036

Style: Colonial
First Floor: 1,540 sq. ft.
Second Floor: 536 sq. ft.
Total: 2,076 sq. ft.
Bonus Space: 502 sq. ft.
Bedrooms: 3
Bathrooms: 2½
Width: 62' - 8"
Depth: 61' - 0"
Foundation: Crawlspace, Basement

SEARCH ONLINE @ EPLANS.COM

FIRST FLOOR

SECOND FLOOR

ORDER BLUEPRINTS 24 HOURS, 7 DAYS A WEEK, AT 1-800-521-6797

plan# HPK0800037

L D

Style: Cape Cod
First Floor: 1,016 sq. ft.
Second Floor: 766 sq. ft.
Total: 1,782 sq. ft.
Bedrooms: 3
Bathrooms: 2½
Width: 33' - 0"
Depth: 30' - 0"
Foundation: Basement

SEARCH ONLINE @ EPLANS.COM

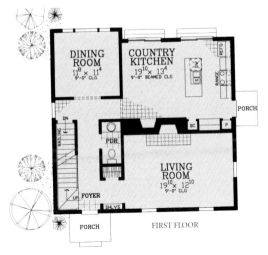

ROOF

BEDROOM
13² × 9⁶

BEDROOM
13⁶ × 9⁶

DN

RAILING

LINEN

MASTER
SUITE
12⁴ × 14²

BATH

BATH DRESSING

SHWR

ROOF

SECOND FLOOR

DINING
ROOM
11⁸ × 11⁴
9'-0" CLG

COUNTRY
KITCHEN
19¹⁰ × 13⁴
9'-0" BEAMED CLG

REFG

RANGE

PORCH

DN

RAILING

PDR.

P

LIVING
ROOM
19¹⁰ × 12¹⁰
9'-0" CLG

UP FOYER

SHLVS.

PORCH

FIRST FLOOR

Here's an expandable Colonial

with a full measure of Cape Cod charm. Salt-box shapes and modular structures popular in Early America enjoyed a revival at the turn of the century and have come to life again—this time with added square footage and some very comfortable amenities. Upstairs, a spacious master suite shares a gallery hall which leads to two family bedrooms and sizable storage space. The expanded version of the basic plan adds a study wing to the left of the foyer as well as an attached garage with a service entrance to the kitchen.

SECOND FLOOR

FIRST FLOOR

ORDER BLUEPRINTS 24 HOURS, 7 DAYS A WEEK, AT 1-800-521-6797

plan # HPK0800040

Style: Colonial
First Floor: 1,211 sq. ft.
Second Floor: 551 sq. ft.
Total: 1,762 sq. ft.
Bonus Space: 378 sq. ft.
Bedrooms: 3
Bathrooms: 2½
Width: 64' - 4"
Depth: 39' - 4"
Foundation: Crawlspace, Basement

SEARCH ONLINE @ EPLANS.COM

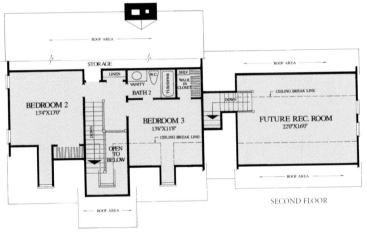

SECOND FLOOR

An endearing and enduring American original that is straightforward and of spare design, yet warm, cozy, and uncomplicated, this home brings the past into sharp focus. The openness of the floor plan pairs the great room with the dining area for convenience and a modern flow. The island kitchen enjoys a view of the front property. The master suite features a large master bath with dual vanities, a compartmented toilet, and separate shower and tub. Two family bedrooms share a bath upstairs. Above the garage is future space that is easily converted into livable space as needed.

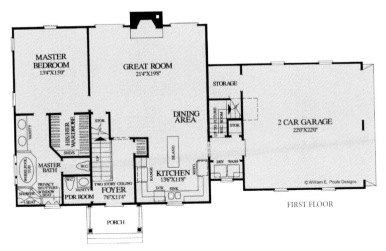

FIRST FLOOR

SECOND FLOOR

FIRST FLOOR

A rear terrace and porch extend the living area and provide ample opportunity for outdoor dining and socializing. Inside, a sunroom offers natural light and a great place to relax any time of day. A first-floor master is a private retreat for the homeowners, conveniently located next to the study. The upgraded laundry room boasts a washer/dryer, deep freezer, built-in ironing board, central table for folding clothes, and a drying closet. A full bath adjacent to the laundry room completes this level. Upstairs houses three additional family bedrooms, three full baths, and a future rec room.

plan# HPK0800042

Style: Colonial
First Floor: 2,092 sq. ft.
Second Floor: 1,045 sq. ft.
Total: 3,137 sq. ft.
Bonus Space: 546 sq. ft.
Bedrooms: 4
Bathrooms: 3½
Width: 56' - 4"
Depth: 52' - 10"
Foundation: Crawlspace

SEARCH ONLINE @ EPLANS.COM

The welcoming charm of this farmhouse is expressed by its many windows and its covered, wraparound porch. A two-story foyer is enhanced by a Palladian window in a clerestory dormer to allow natural lighting. A first-floor master suite allows privacy and accessibility. The master bath includes a whirlpool tub, separate shower, and double-bowl vanity, along with a walk-in closet. The second floor provides two additional bedrooms, a full bath, and plenty of storage space.

SECOND FLOOR

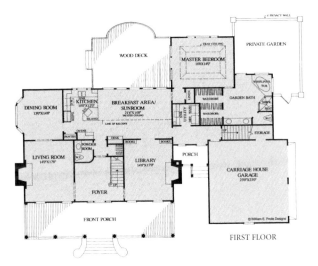

FIRST FLOOR

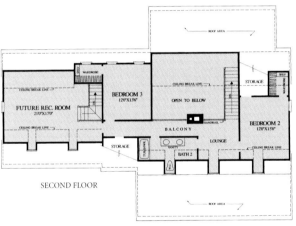

SECOND FLOOR

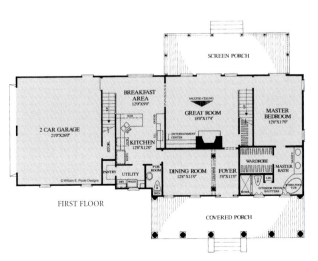

FIRST FLOOR

plan# HPK0800043

Style: Colonial
First Floor: 1,370 sq. ft.
Second Floor: 668 sq. ft.
Total: 2,038 sq. ft.
Bonus Space: 421 sq. ft.
Bedrooms: 3
Bathrooms: 2½
Width: 71' - 8"
Depth: 49' - 4"
Foundation: Crawlspace

SEARCH ONLINE @ EPLANS.COM

This charming 1½-story home

offers an inviting front porch and a rear screened porch, increasing the living space significantly. The foyer opens to the formal dining room and the great room, which in turn leads to the screened porch. The master suite is tucked away for privacy on the right—the sunny bedroom adjoins a luxurious private bath. The second-floor balcony, full bath, and lounge area separate the two family bedrooms.

plan # HPK0800044

Style: Colonial
Square Footage: 2,595
Bonus Space: 1,480 sq. ft.
Bedrooms: 4
Bathrooms: 2½
Width: 78' - 8"
Depth: 67' - 0"
Foundation: Basement

SEARCH ONLINE @ EPLANS.COM

This home has a touch of modernism with all the comforts of country style. The pillared front porch allows for summer evening relaxation. The foyer extends into the bright great room equipped with a fireplace. The large kitchen is stationed between the vaulted dining room and airy breakfast nook. Two walk-in closets, dual vanities, and a spacious bath complement the master suite. Each of the three family bedrooms features closet space. The entire second floor is left for future development, whether it be a guest room, rec room, or study—or all three.

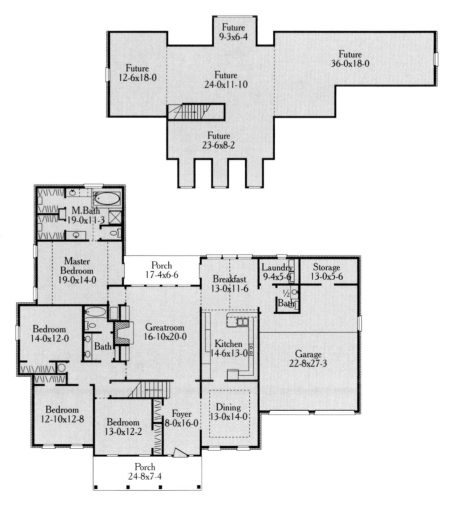

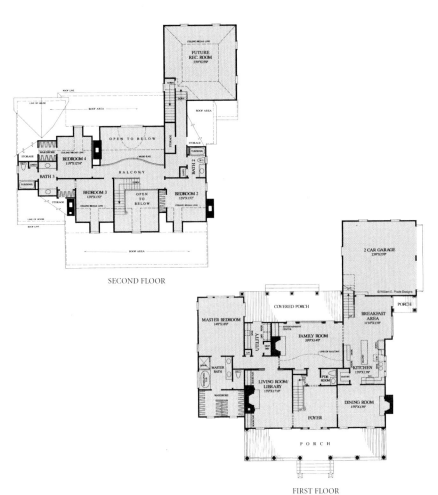

SECOND FLOOR

FIRST FLOOR

plan# HPK0800045

Style: Colonial
First Floor: 2,200 sq. ft.
Second Floor: 1,001 sq. ft.
Total: 3,201 sq. ft.
Bonus Space: 674 sq. ft.
Bedrooms: 4
Bathrooms: 3½
Width: 70' - 4"
Depth: 74' - 4"
Foundation: Crawlspace

SEARCH ONLINE @ EPLANS.COM

A wide, welcoming front porch and three dormer windows lend Southern flair to this charming farmhouse. Inside, three fireplaces—found in the living, dining, and family rooms—create a cozy atmosphere. The family room opens to the covered rear porch, and the breakfast area opens to a small side porch. Sleeping quarters include a luxurious first-floor master suite—with a private bath and two walk-in closets—as well as three family bedrooms upstairs.

EARLY AMERICAN GEORGIANS

Georgian-style homes gained popularity in the early- to mid-18th Century, an early twist on the first Colonial homes. The style caught on quickly and was far-reaching, spreading up and down the Eastern seaboard from what is now Maine to Georgia. It remains popular today, one of the most enduring architectural styles of the Colonial period.

Typically two stories, Georgians can be most easily identified by their elaborate entryways. A paneled front door features a decorative crown, and is supported by pilasters on each side. The crown could be wood, brick, or stone, depending on the building material used for the home. Above the door—or occasionally within it—a row of rectangular windows just beneath the crown adds additional decoration.

Other defining characteristics of the Georgian style included a cornice with decorative wood moldings and double-hung windows with small panes separated by wooden muntins.

Georgians were built with a variety of roof styles, which typically varied by region. The most common, as reflected in the homes in this chapter, is the side-gabled roof. Others featured gambrel or hipped roofs, or a centered gable on the front facade.■

A front-facing gable adds to the impressive entryway on Design HPK0800057 (page 60).

QUOTE ONE®

SECOND FLOOR

FIRST FLOOR

plan# HPK0800046

Style: Georgian
First Floor: 1,554 sq. ft.
Second Floor: 1,648 sq. ft.
Total: 3,202 sq. ft.
Bedrooms: 4
Bathrooms: 3½
Width: 60' - 0"
Depth: 43' - 0"
Foundation: Walkout Basement

SEARCH ONLINE @ EPLANS.COM

The classic styling of this brick American traditional home will be respected for years to come. The formidable, double-door, transomed entry and a Palladian window reveal the shining foyer within. The spacious dining room and the formal study or living room flank the foyer; a large family room with a full wall of glass conveniently opens to the breakfast room and the kitchen. The master suite features a spacious sitting area with its own fireplace and a tray ceiling. Two additional bedrooms share a bath, and a fourth bedroom has its own private bath.

ORDER BLUEPRINTS 24 HOURS, 7 DAYS A WEEK, AT 1-800-521-6797

plan# HPK0800047

Style: Georgian
First Floor: 1,930 sq. ft.
Second Floor: 1,807 sq. ft.
Total: 3,737 sq. ft.
Bonus Space: 372 sq. ft.
Bedrooms: 3
Bathrooms: 4
Width: 55' - 2"
Depth: 60' - 2"
Foundation: Crawlspace

SEARCH ONLINE @ EPLANS.COM

Classic Georgian stylings create a stately feel on this brick two-story home. A portico entry leads to a gracious foyer and formal rooms on either side. Ahead, a guest suite/home office has a semi-private bath. The kitchen aims to please with a large serving bar island and plenty of counter space. A casual breakfast nook and hearth-warmed gathering room with deck access complete this level. Upstairs, two bedrooms share a Jack-and-Jill bath, and the bonus room contains an additional full bath. The master suite is a remarkable getaway, with a tray ceiling, His and Hers walk-in closets, and an opulent bath with an elegant ceiling treatment. A laundry room nearby is the ultimate convenience.

FIRST FLOOR

SECOND FLOOR

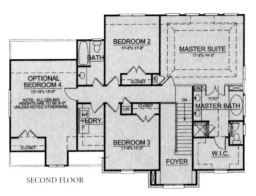

SECOND FLOOR

FIRST FLOOR

STOOP

plan # HPK0800048

Style: Georgian
First Floor: 943 sq. ft.
Second Floor: 1,122 sq. ft.
Total: 2,065 sq. ft.
Bonus Space: 289 sq. ft.
Bedrooms: 3
Bathrooms: 2½
Width: 50' - 0"
Depth: 35' - 0"
Foundation: Basement

SEARCH ONLINE @ EPLANS.COM

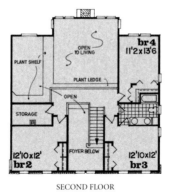

SECOND FLOOR

plan # HPK0800049

Style: Georgian
First Floor: 1,929 sq. ft.
Second Floor: 975 sq. ft.
Total: 2,904 sq. ft.
Bedrooms: 4
Bathrooms: 2½
Width: 64' - 8"
Depth: 49' - 6"
Foundation: Basement, Crawlspace

SEARCH ONLINE @ EPLANS.COM

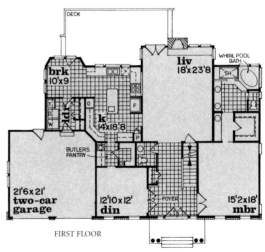

FIRST FLOOR

plan ⊕ HPK0800050

Style: Georgian
First Floor: 1,370 sq. ft.
Second Floor: 1,381 sq. ft.
Total: 2,751 sq. ft.
Bedrooms: 4
Bathrooms: 3½
Width: 52' - 2"
Depth: 55' - 6"
Foundation: Crawlspace

SEARCH ONLINE @ EPLANS.COM

If you are looking for a classic home with timeless appeal and historic style, this design will make those dreams come true. Enter to a formal foyer; on the right, a hearth-warmed gathering room is a comfortable place to relax. To the left, the living room enjoys natural light from a bay window and flows into the dining room through a columned archway. The kitchen is bright and open and easily serves the quaint breakfast nook. On the upper level, three generous bedrooms (one with a private bath) join the beautifully appointed master suite and share a light-filled sitting area.

SECOND FLOOR

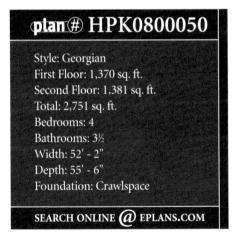

FIRST FLOOR

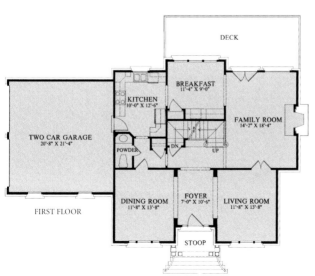

SECOND FLOOR

plan# HPK0800051

Style: Georgian
First Floor: 1,165 sq. ft.
Second Floor: 1,050 sq. ft.
Total: 2,215 sq. ft.
Bonus Space: 265 sq. ft.
Bedrooms: 3
Bathrooms: 2½
Width: 58' - 0"
Depth: 36' - 0"
Foundation: Walkout Basement

SEARCH ONLINE @ EPLANS.COM

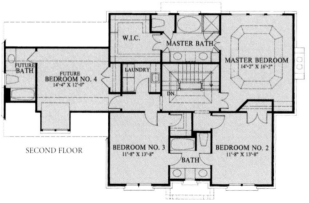

FIRST FLOOR

No detail is left to chance in this classically designed two-story home. A formal entry opens to the living and dining rooms through graceful arches. For more casual entertaining, the family room provides ample space for large gatherings and features a warming fireplace and access to the rear deck through double doors. The adjacent L-shaped kitchen handles any occasion with ease. Upstairs, the master suite runs the width of the house and includes a generous walk-in closet and a bath with a knee-space vanity, twin lavatories, a garden tub, and a separate shower. A central hall leads to two family bedrooms and a full bath, as well as bonus space, which offers the possibility of a future fourth bedroom and bath.

© Stephen Fuller, Inc.

plan # HPK0800052

Style: Georgian
First Floor: 1,787 sq. ft.
Second Floor: 851 sq. ft.
Total: 2,638 sq. ft.
Bonus Space: 189 sq. ft.
Bedrooms: 3
Bathrooms: 2½
Width: 51' - 3"
Depth: 70' - 6"
Foundation: Walkout Basement

SEARCH ONLINE @ EPLANS.COM

This beautiful brick design displays fine family livability in over 2,600 square feet. The wraparound porch welcomes family and friends to inside living areas. The great room sports an elegant ceiling, a fireplace, and built-ins. The kitchen displays good traffic patterning. An island cooktop will please the house gourmet. The dining room features double doors that open out onto the porch. In the master bedroom, a pampering bath includes a whirlpool tub and separate vanities. A walk-in closet is located at the back of the bath. Two family bedrooms upstairs enjoy peace and quiet and a full hall bath with natural illumination.

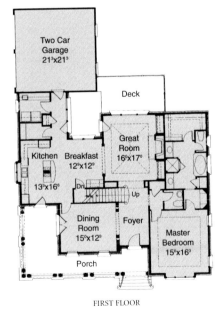

FIRST FLOOR

SECOND FLOOR

The charm of this home is evident from the moment you step onto the front porch. The family room stretches from front to back porches and delights with its central hearth. For formal occasions, the living room combines with the dining room to create the perfect atmosphere. The U-shaped kitchen serves the breakfast room. In the second-floor master suite, double doors lead to the formal bath. It features angled vanities and a whirlpool tub. An unfinished bonus area opens at the rear. Two secondary bedrooms share a bath.

plan# HPK0800053

Style: Georgian
First Floor: 1,609 sq. ft.
Second Floor: 1,583 sq. ft.
Total: 3,192 sq. ft.
Bonus Space: 126 sq. ft.
Bedrooms: 3
Bathrooms: 2½
Width: 49' - 3"
Depth: 73' - 0"
Foundation: Walkout Basement

SEARCH ONLINE @ EPLANS.COM

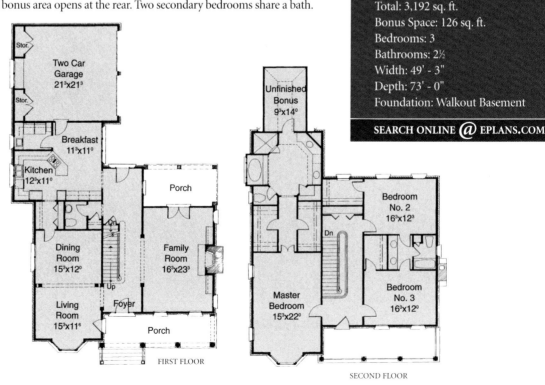

FIRST FLOOR

SECOND FLOOR

ORDER BLUEPRINTS 24 HOURS, 7 DAYS A WEEK, AT 1-800-521-6797

plan# HPK0800054

Style: Georgian
First Floor: 1,501 sq. ft.
Second Floor: 1,252 sq. ft.
Total: 2,753 sq. ft.
Bedrooms: 3
Bathrooms: 2½
Width: 46' - 3"
Depth: 76' - 9"
Foundation: Walkout Basement

SEARCH ONLINE @ EPLANS.COM

A covered porch provides a warm welcome to this graceful, brick traditional home. The foyer opens on the right to the family room with a warming fireplace and on the left to the formal living and dining areas. To the rear of the plan, the U-shaped island kitchen offers an abundance of work and storage space and is joined with the breakfast room. The second floor contains the sleeping area. The master suite is enhanced by a romantic fireplace, luxurious bath, and huge walk-in closet. Two family bedrooms privately share a full bath.

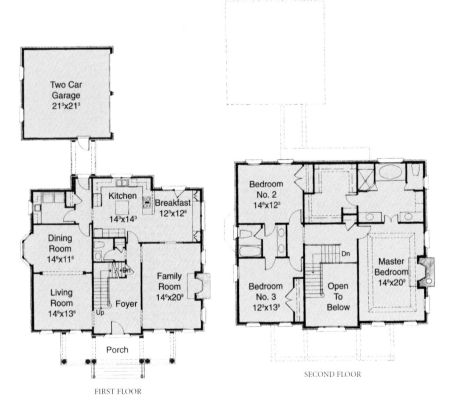

Two Car Garage 21³x21³

Kitchen 14³x14³

Breakfast 12³x12⁶

Dining Room 14⁶x11⁶

Living Room 14⁶x13⁶

Foyer

Family Room 14⁶x20⁹

Porch

FIRST FLOOR

Bedroom No. 2 14⁶x12³

Bedroom No. 3 12³x13⁶

Open To Below

Dn

Master Bedroom 14⁶x20⁹

SECOND FLOOR

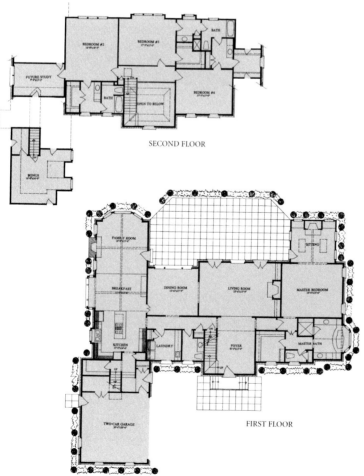

SECOND FLOOR

FIRST FLOOR

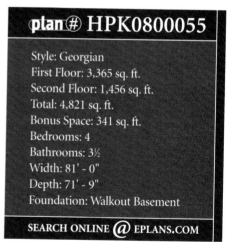

plan # HPK0800055

Style: Georgian
First Floor: 3,365 sq. ft.
Second Floor: 1,456 sq. ft.
Total: 4,821 sq. ft.
Bonus Space: 341 sq. ft.
Bedrooms: 4
Bathrooms: 3½
Width: 81' - 0"
Depth: 71' - 9"
Foundation: Walkout Basement

SEARCH ONLINE @ EPLANS.COM

The graceful lines of this formal Georgian brick manor are an inviting presence in any neighborhood. An open foyer enjoys views of the back property through the living room, which features a fireplace framed with built-in bookshelves. Dinner guests will want to linger on the rear terrace, which opens through French doors from formal and casual areas. The gourmet kitchen has a cooktop island, a walk-in pantry and a breakfast area that's open to the bright family room. Homeowners will enjoy the master bedroom's private sitting area, which features two skylights, a fireplace, and access to the terrace.

plan# HPK0800056

Style: Georgian
First Floor: 2,183 sq. ft.
Second Floor: 993 sq. ft.
Total: 3,176 sq. ft.
Bedrooms: 4
Bathrooms: 3½
Width: 66' - 0"
Depth: 84' - 0"
Foundation: Slab

SEARCH ONLINE @ EPLANS.COM

This home combines French styling with Colonial influences to produce a magnificent picture of elegance. A grand two-story foyer introduces the living room to the left and the dining room to the right. The family room reveals a fireplace flanked by two sets of French doors leading to the rear porch. The island kitchen provides plenty of workspace and functions well with a breakfast room, a convenient utility room, and a powder room. The first-floor master suite is a secluded place to relax. Upstairs, three family bedrooms—all with walk-in closets—and two full baths complete the sleeping quarters. An unfinished bonus room above the two-car garage is great for future space.

REAR EXTERIOR

FIRST FLOOR

SECOND FLOOR

SECOND FLOOR

ATTIC STORAGE

BEDROOM 15⁰x11⁴

BEDROOM 10⁴x13⁴

BATH

TUB

BATH

UP

VANITY

DRESSING RM.

VANITY

LINEN

WALK-IN CLOSET

BEDROOM 15⁰x11⁴

OPEN STAIR WELL

MASTER BEDROOM 14⁰x18⁰

LOUNGE 21⁰x11⁸

ROOF

ROOF

ROOF

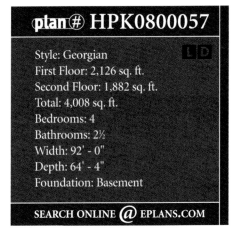

QUOTE ONE®

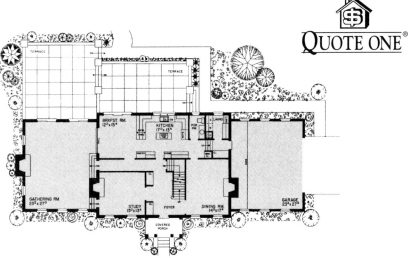

FIRST FLOOR

TERRACE

TERRACE

BRKFST. RM. 12⁴x13⁴

KITCHEN 17⁰x13⁴

POP

LAUND.

PANTRY

GATHERING RM. 23⁵x27⁰

STUDY 15⁰x13⁴

FOYER

DINING RM. 14⁰x17⁰

GARAGE 23⁴x27⁰

COVERED PORCH

plan # HPK0800057

Style: Georgian
First Floor: 2,126 sq. ft.
Second Floor: 1,882 sq. ft.
Total: 4,008 sq. ft.
Bedrooms: 4
Bathrooms: 2½
Width: 92' - 0"
Depth: 64' - 4"
Foundation: Basement

SEARCH ONLINE @ EPLANS.COM

This historical Georgian home has its roots in the 18th Century. The full two-story center section is delightfully complemented by the one-and-a-half-story wings. An elegant gathering room, three steps down from the rest of the house, provides ample space for entertaining on a grand scale. The study and the formal dining room flank the foyer. Each of these rooms has a fireplace as its highlight. The breakfast room, kitchen, powder room, and laundry room are arranged for maximum efficiency. The second floor houses the family bedrooms. Take special note of the spacious master suite.

SECOND FLOOR

plan # HPK0800058

Style: Georgian
First Floor: 2,798 sq. ft.
Second Floor: 1,496 sq. ft.
Total: 4,294 sq. ft.
Bonus Space: 515 sq. ft.
Bedrooms: 4
Bathrooms: 3½
Width: 91' - 10"
Depth: 57' - 2"
Foundation: Crawlspace, Basement

SEARCH ONLINE @ EPLANS.COM

FIRST FLOOR

This classic Georgian design captures old-world charm with modern amenities. A spacious library boasts a built-in bookcase and central fireplace. A second fireplace warms the family room, large island-kitchen and breakfast area. Convenient access to the rear porch makes outdoor dining an option. A private elevator takes luxury to new heights. Once upstairs, bedroom #2—enhanced by a personal fireplace—is outfitted with a built-in bookcase, a huge wardrobe, a spacious storage area, and a full bath with whirlpool tub. Two additional family bedrooms share a full bath. An expansive rec room completes this level. Extra storage space in the garage is an addded bonus.

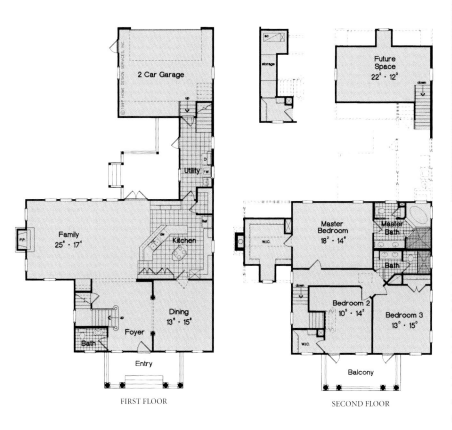

FIRST FLOOR

SECOND FLOOR

plan# HPK0800059

Style: Georgian
First Floor: 1,447 sq. ft.
Second Floor: 1,423 sq. ft.
Total: 2,870 sq. ft.
Bonus Space: 264 sq. ft.
Bedrooms: 3
Bathrooms: 2½
Width: 45' - 0"
Depth: 80' - 0"
Foundation: Slab

SEARCH ONLINE @ EPLANS.COM

This grand home delights with its beautiful Greek Revival facade. The magnificent portico offers a balcony that is accessible to Bedrooms 2 and 3. The foyer opens to the family room with its window wall and fireplace. The angled kitchen is sure to please with its proximity to the laundry room. Upstairs is the master suite, designed to pamper with a delightful private bath and walk-in closet. Bedrooms 2 and 3 share a full bath and balcony. Bonus space is available for future expansion above the two-car garage.

plan# HPK0800060

Style: Georgian
First Floor: 1,760 sq. ft.
Second Floor: 2,001 sq. ft.
Total: 3,761 sq. ft.
Bonus Space: 448 sq. ft.
Bedrooms: 3
Bathrooms: 3½
Width: 99' - 1"
Depth: 57' - 9"
Foundation: Basement

SEARCH ONLINE @ EPLANS.COM

Stately gentility is a most appropriate phrase for this dignified Georgian design. The brick finish on the exterior is further enhanced by the cut-stone trim and the twin brick chimneys venting the multiple fireplaces. The large formal entry is an elegant setting for the four-foot-wide main stair—only one of three stairs that gives this home a well-thought-out traffic pattern. This home has all of the amenities that the most discerning homeowner could want. Note the generous family room, the island kitchen, and the adjoining rear porch for comfortable informal living. The second floor has one of the most luxurious master suites. It features His and Hers dressing areas, a fireplace, and even a petit dejeuner for late night snacks. Don't overlook the possibilities for the future living spaces in the lower level and over the carriage house.

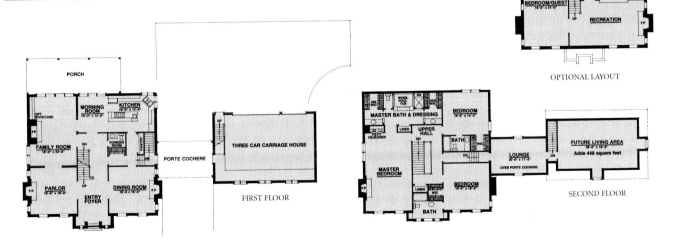

OPTIONAL LAYOUT

FIRST FLOOR

SECOND FLOOR

SECOND FLOOR

FIRST FLOOR

plan# HPK0800061

Style: Georgian
First Floor: 2,767 sq. ft.
Second Floor: 1,179 sq. ft.
Total: 3,946 sq. ft.
Bonus Space: 591 sq. ft.
Bedrooms: 4
Bathrooms: 3½ + ½
Width: 79' - 11"
Depth: 80' - 6"
Foundation: Crawlspace

SEARCH ONLINE @ EPLANS.COM

Memories of Christmas at home with the large tree greeting you upon entering the gracious foyer, garland hanging along the curved staircase, carols being sung around the piano in the library, turkey and pumpkin pie baking in the kitchen—these are what the Evergreen is all about. With the curved and columned front porch, authentic detail, and gracious flow, family and neighbors gather with joy in this 'home for all seasons' throughout the year and especially for holidays.

ORDER BLUEPRINTS 24 HOURS, 7 DAYS A WEEK, AT 1-800-521-6797

plan# HPK0800062

Style: Georgian
First Floor: 2,173 sq. ft.
Second Floor: 986 sq. ft.
Total: 3,159 sq. ft.
Bedrooms: 4
Bathrooms: 3½
Width: 67' - 0"
Depth: 54' - 0"
Foundation: Basement

SEARCH ONLINE @ EPLANS.COM

This traditional home features an elegant facade enhanced by Neoclassical details. A front portico welcomes you inside to a two-story foyer flanked by a formal parlor and a dining room. Straight ahead, a stunning circular staircase dominates the center of the plan. The two-story grand room features a fireplace, and the kitchen offers a cooking island and morning nook. The keeping room accesses the rear deck. The first-floor master suite is impressive with a private bath and double walk-in closet. A three-car garage and laundry room complete the first floor. Upstairs, Bedroom 2 provides a private bath, while Bedrooms 3 and 4 share a Jack-and-Jill bath.

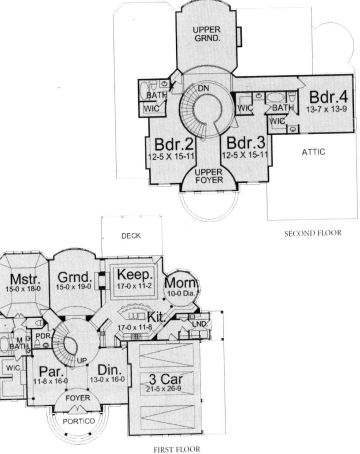

SECOND FLOOR

FIRST FLOOR

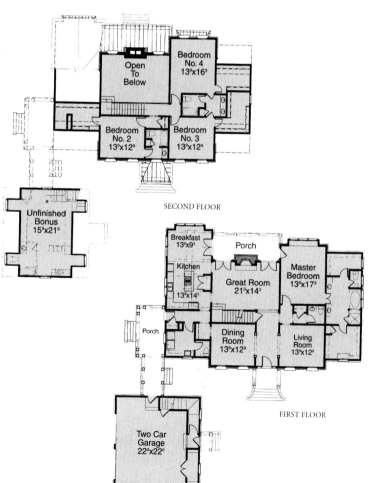

SECOND FLOOR

FIRST FLOOR

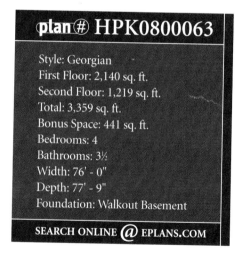

plan# HPK0800063

Style: Georgian
First Floor: 2,140 sq. ft.
Second Floor: 1,219 sq. ft.
Total: 3,359 sq. ft.
Bonus Space: 441 sq. ft.
Bedrooms: 4
Bathrooms: 3½
Width: 76' - 0"
Depth: 77' - 9"
Foundation: Walkout Basement

SEARCH ONLINE @ EPLANS.COM

With its adjacent two-car garage connected to the main house via a covered walkway and porch, this design would make an excellent home for a corner lot. Inside the main house, the entry leads to a formal living room, a formal dining room, and a massive great room with a fireplace flanked by French doors to the rear porch. The island kitchen includes a large pantry and a breakfast nook with outdoor access. The master bedroom is found on the first floor for privacy and features a luxurious private bath. Three bedrooms, all with large walk-in closets, and two full baths are located upstairs. Additional bonus space is available over the garage for a guest suite or a game room.

ORDER BLUEPRINTS 24 HOURS, 7 DAYS A WEEK, AT 1-800-521-6797

plan # HPK0800064

Style: Georgian
First Floor: 2,603 sq. ft.
Second Floor: 1,660 sq. ft.
Total: 4,263 sq. ft.
Bonus Space: 669 sq. ft.
Bedrooms: 4
Bathrooms: 4½ + ½
Width: 98' - 0"
Depth: 56' - 8"
Foundation: Basement

SEARCH ONLINE @ EPLANS.COM

This fine example of the Georgian style of architecture offers a wonderful facade with Southern charm. The foyer is flanked by the formal dining room and the living room. The efficient kitchen is situated between the sunny breakfast nook and the dining room. The family room opens to the backyard. The master suite enjoys an opulent bath and large walk-in closet. The second floor presents three bedrooms and two baths.

SECOND FLOOR

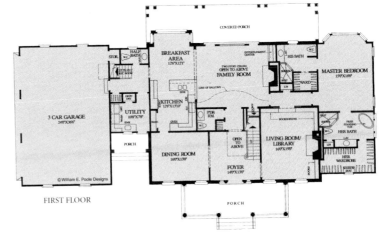

FIRST FLOOR

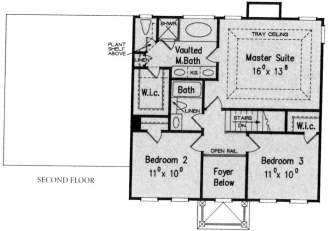

SECOND FLOOR

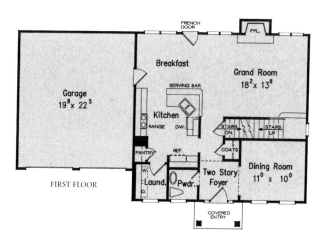

FIRST FLOOR

plan# HPK0800065

Style: Georgian
First Floor: 840 sq. ft.
Second Floor: 766 sq. ft.
Total: 1,606 sq. ft.
Bedrooms: 3
Bathrooms: 2½
Width: 50' - 0"
Depth: 34' - 4"
Foundation: Crawlspace, Basement

SEARCH ONLINE @ EPLANS.COM

Gabled dormers, keystone lintels, and a covered entry display a pleasant exterior. Inside, the kitchen and breakfast area opens to the grand room, which features a warming fireplace. A powder room is located just across from the dining room. On the second floor, three bedrooms provide plenty of room for the family, including the master suite with a vaulted private bath and a large walk-in closet. Don't miss the two-car garage that enters through the breakfast area.

ORDER BLUEPRINTS 24 HOURS, 7 DAYS A WEEK, AT 1-800-521-6797

plan ⊕ HPK0800066

Style: Georgian
First Floor: 2,168 sq. ft.
Second Floor: 1,203 sq. ft.
Total: 3,371 sq. ft.
Bonus Space: 452 sq. ft.
Bedrooms: 4
Bathrooms: 4½
Width: 71' - 2"
Depth: 63' - 4"
Foundation: Crawlspace, Basement

SEARCH ONLINE @ EPLANS.COM

SECOND FLOOR

FIRST FLOOR

This stately two-story beauty offers the utmost in style and livability. The grand columned entryway is topped by a railed roof, making it the centerpiece of the facade. Formal space resides at the front of the plan, with a living room and dining room flanking the foyer. Secluded behind the staircase is the elegant master suite, with a huge walk-in closet and swanky private bath. The hearth-warmed family room flows into the island kitchen and breakfast nook, making this space the comfortable hub of home life. A laundry room and half-bath are convenient to this area. Upstairs, three bedrooms all have access to separate baths and share space with a future recreation room.

SECOND FLOOR

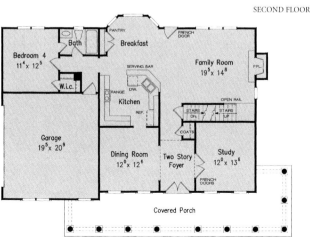

FIRST FLOOR

A Southern classic, this lovely home will become a treasured place to call your own. The entry makes a grand impression; double doors open to the foyer where French doors reveal a study. To the right, the dining room is designed for entertaining, with easy access to the angled serving-bar kitchen. A bayed breakfast nook leads into the hearth-warmed family room. Tucked to the rear, a bedroom with a full bath makes an ideal guest room. The master suite is upstairs and enjoys a private vaulted spa bath. Two additional bedrooms reside on this level and join a full bath and an optional bonus room, perfect as a kid's retreat, home gym, or crafts room.

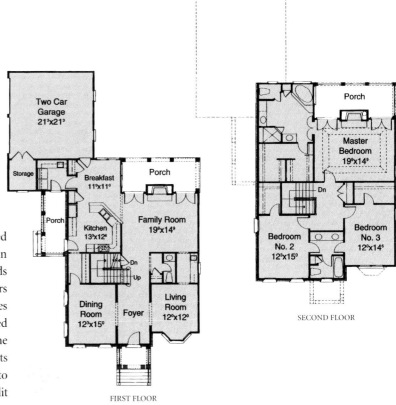

plan # HPK0800068

Style: Georgian
First Floor: 1,465 sq. ft.
Second Floor: 1,332 sq. ft.
Total: 2,797 sq. ft.
Bedrooms: 3
Bathrooms: 2½
Width: 49' - 0"
Depth: 75' - 0"
Foundation: Walkout Basement

SEARCH ONLINE @ EPLANS.COM

Brick, horizontal siding, and a columned porch add elements of style to this graceful Georgian Revival design. Formal rooms flank the foyer, which leads to casual living space with a fireplace and French doors to the rear porch. A convenient butler's pantry eases service to the dining room from the well-planned kitchen. Angled counter space allows an overlook to the breakfast room. Upstairs, a rambling master suite has its own hearth and two sets of French doors that lead out to a private porch. The homeowner's bath features a split walk-in closet, an angled shower, a whirlpool tub, and a compartmented bath. Each of two family bedrooms enjoys private access to a shared bath.

FIRST FLOOR

SECOND FLOOR

The double wings, twin chimneys, and center portico of this home work in concert to create a classic architectural statement. The two-story foyer is flanked by the spacious dining room and formal living room, each containing their own fireplaces. A large family room with a full wall of glass opens conveniently to the kitchen and breakfast room. The master suite features a tray ceiling and French doors that open to a covered porch. A grand master bath completes the master suite. Two family bedrooms share a bath, and another has a private bath. Bedroom 4 features a nook for sitting or reading.

plan # HPK0800069

Style: Georgian
First Floor: 1,455 sq. ft.
Second Floor: 1,649 sq. ft.
Total: 3,104 sq. ft.
Bedrooms: 4
Bathrooms: 3½
Width: 54' - 4"
Depth: 46' - 0"
Foundation: Walkout Basement

SEARCH ONLINE @ EPLANS.COM

FIRST FLOOR

SECOND FLOOR

ORDER BLUEPRINTS 24 HOURS, 7 DAYS A WEEK, AT 1-800-521-6797

plan# HPK0800070

Style: Georgian
First Floor: 2,081 sq. ft.
Second Floor: 940 sq. ft.
Total: 3,021 sq. ft.
Bedrooms: 4
Bathrooms: 3½
Width: 69' - 9"
Depth: 65' - 0"
Foundation: Walkout Basement

SEARCH ONLINE @ EPLANS.COM

SECOND FLOOR

This Georgian country-style home displays an impressive appearance. The front porch and columns frame the elegant elliptical entrance. Georgian symmetry balances the living room and dining room off the foyer. The first floor continues into the two-story great room, which offers built-in cabinetry, a fireplace, and a large bay window that overlooks the rear deck. A dramatic tray ceiling, a wall of glass, and access to the rear deck complete the master bedroom. To the left of the great room, a large kitchen opens to a breakfast area with walls of windows. Upstairs, each of three family bedrooms features ample closet space as well as direct access to a bathroom.

FIRST FLOOR

The elegant entry of this Colonial home gives it a stately appearance with its columns and pediment. Inside, the entry opens to the living room where the first of two fireplaces is found. The formal dining room adjoins both the living room and the kitchen. The spacious breakfast area looks out onto the patio. The master suite is found on the right with two additional bedrooms, and a fourth bedroom is on the left, giving privacy for overnight guests.

plan# HPK0800071

Style: Georgian
Square Footage: 3,136
Bedrooms: 4
Bathrooms: 3½
Width: 80' - 6"
Depth: 72' - 4"
Foundation: Crawlspace

SEARCH ONLINE @ EPLANS.COM

ORDER BLUEPRINTS 24 HOURS, 7 DAYS A WEEK, AT 1-800-521-6797

© William E. Poole Designs

plan# HPK0800072

Style: Georgian
Square Footage: 3,600
Bedrooms: 4
Bathrooms: 3½
Width: 76' - 2"
Depth: 100' - 10"
Foundation: Crawlspace, Basement

SEARCH ONLINE @ EPLANS.COM

plan# HPK0800073

Style: Georgian
Square Footage: 4,646
Bedrooms: 3
Bathrooms: 3½
Width: 111' - 10"
Depth: 76' - 0"
Foundation: Walkout Basement

SEARCH ONLINE @ EPLANS.COM

This attractive Georgian-inspired home incorporates a classic look with modern amenities for a family home that is sure to please. Follow a 14-foot ceiling from the foyer into the great room, where a warming fireplace is framed by radius windows. A creative use of counter space places the kitchen between the dining room, with decorative columns and a box-bay window, and the sunny breakfast nook. Two bedrooms on this side of the home share a full hall bath. On the far left, the master suite reigns. The bedroom is surrounded by luxurious touches, including an octagonal tray ceiling and an arched opening to the sitting room. In the vaulted bath, a garden tub will relax any stress away.

plan# HPK0800074

Style: Georgian
Square Footage: 1,768
Bonus Space: 347 sq. ft.
Bedrooms: 3
Bathrooms: 2
Width: 54' - 0"
Depth: 59' - 6"
Foundation: Crawlspace, Slab

SEARCH ONLINE @ EPLANS.COM

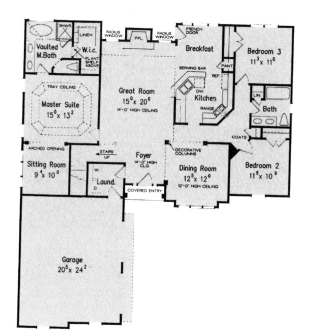

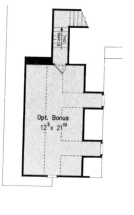

ORDER BLUEPRINTS 24 HOURS, 7 DAYS A WEEK, AT 1-800-521-6797

plan# HPK0800075

Style: Georgian
First Floor: 1,217 sq. ft.
Second Floor: 1,390 sq. ft.
Total: 2,607 sq. ft.
Bedrooms: 5
Bathrooms: 3
Width: 50' - 0"
Depth: 40' - 4"
Foundation: Basement,
Crawlspace, Slab

SEARCH ONLINE @ EPLANS.COM

Enter this beautiful five-bedroom Georgian home and you may never want to leave! An elegant, open floor plan reveals a family room, with a fireplace, leading to the breakfast area and U-shaped island kitchen. Upstairs, the master suite will amaze, with a sitting room, luxurious vaulted bath, and a walk-in closet so huge you have to see it to believe it! Three ample family bedrooms share a full bath. Don't miss the upper-level laundry room, positioned for ultimate convenience.

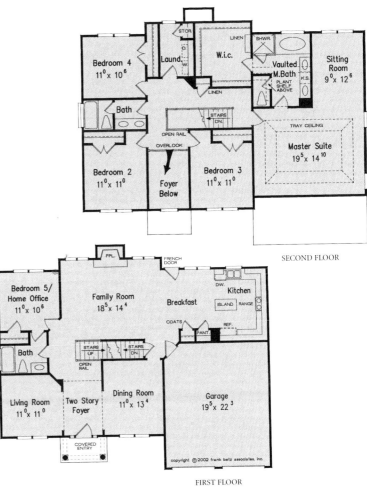

SECOND FLOOR

FIRST FLOOR

Your future dream home awaits in this Early American Georgian design. Once inside, you are immediately enveloped by a sense of spaciousness. The open layout of the dining room and parlor follows the trend of informality in living areas. A guest room to the left enjoys a private entrance to a full bath. A fireplace in the living room warms the adjacent breakfast nook and island-cooktop kitchen. Upstairs, the master bedroom's intricate design, enhanced by tray ceilings, features a sitting area, a roomy bath, and a large walk-in closet with two entrances. Three additional family bedrooms and two full baths complete the second floor.

plan# HPK0800076

Style: Georgian
First Floor: 1,813 sq. ft.
Second Floor: 1,441 sq. ft.
Total: 3,254 sq. ft.
Bedrooms: 5
Bathrooms: 4
Width: 49' - 0"
Depth: 59' - 0"
Foundation: Basement

SEARCH ONLINE @ EPLANS.COM

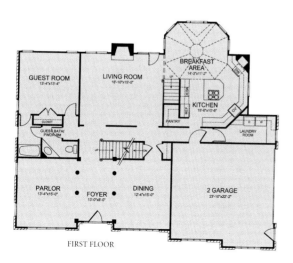

FIRST FLOOR

SECOND FLOOR

plan# HPK0800077

Style: Georgian
First Floor: 2,253 sq. ft.
Second Floor: 890 sq. ft.
Total: 3,143 sq. ft.
Bedrooms: 4
Bathrooms: 3½
Width: 61' - 6"
Depth: 64' - 0"
Foundation: Basement

SEARCH ONLINE @ EPLANS.COM

REAR EXTERIOR

SECOND FLOOR

FIRST FLOOR

This grand Georgian home begins with a double-door entry topped by a beautiful arched window. Inside, the foyer opens to the two-story living room, which has a wide bow window overlooking the rear property. Double doors open to a study warmed by a fireplace. The kitchen features a walk-in pantry and serves both the formal dining room and the breakfast area, which adjoins the bright keeping room. The master suite, secluded on the first floor, is large and opulent. Three more bedrooms and two baths are upstairs for family and friends.

PHOTO BY EXPOSURES UNLIMITED, RON & DONNA KOLB

THIS HOME, AS SHOWN IN THE PHOTOGRAPH, MAY DIFFER FROM THE ACTUAL BLUEPRINTS

SECOND FLOOR

FIRST FLOOR

plan# HPK0800078

Style: Georgian
First Floor: 1,759 sq. ft.
Second Floor: 1,607 sq. ft.
Total: 3,366 sq. ft.
Bedrooms: 5
Bathrooms: 4
Width: 68' - 8"
Depth: 56' - 8"
Foundation: Basement

SEARCH ONLINE @ EPLANS.COM

This luxurious two-story home combines a stately Williamsburg exterior style with a large, functional floor plan. Natural light radiates through the multiple rear windows to flood the great room, breakfast area, and kitchen. Secluded to the rear of this home is an optional library or bedroom, which can serve as a comfortable guest room. Built-in bookshelves flank the entrance to the second-floor master bedroom where a lavish retreat offers a large sitting area surrounded by windows. Three additional bedrooms, each with large closets and private access to a bath, complete this family-friendly home.

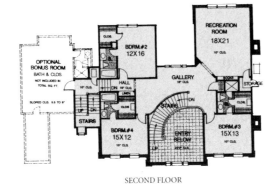

plan# HPK0800079

Style: Georgian
First Floor: 3,599 sq. ft.
Second Floor: 1,621 sq. ft.
Total: 5,220 sq. ft.
Bonus Space: 537 sq. ft.
Bedrooms: 4
Bathrooms: 5½
Width: 108' - 10"
Depth: 53' - 10"
Foundation: Slab, Basement

SEARCH ONLINE @ EPLANS.COM

A grand facade detailed with brick corner
quoins, stucco flourishes, arched windows, and an elegant entrance presents this home. A spacious foyer is
accented by curving stairs and flanked by a formal
living room and a formal dining room. For cozy
times, a through-fireplace is located between a large
family room and a quiet study. The master bedroom
is designed to pamper, with two walk-in closets, a
two-sided fireplace, a bayed sitting area, and a lavish
private bath. Upstairs, three secondary bedrooms
each have a private bath and a walk-in closet. Also on
this level is a spacious recreation room, perfect for a
game room or children's playroom.

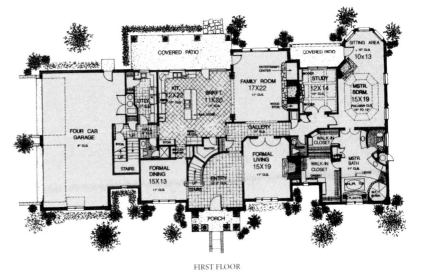

SECOND FLOOR

FIRST FLOOR

SECOND FLOOR

FIRST FLOOR

QUOTE ONE®

plan# HPK0800080

Style: Georgian
First Floor: 1,370 sq. ft.
Second Floor: 1,673 sq. ft.
Total: 3,043 sq. ft.
Bedrooms: 4
Bathrooms: 3½
Width: 73' - 6"
Depth: 49' - 0"
Foundation: Walkout Basement

SEARCH ONLINE @ EPLANS.COM

This English Georgian home exhibits a dramatic brick exterior. Enter the two-story foyer—the unusually shaped staircase and balcony overlook create a tremendous first impression. Separated only by a classical colonnade detail, the living and dining rooms are perfect for entertaining. The great room features a fireplace on the outside wall. This room opens to the breakfast room and angled kitchen with plenty of cabinets and counter space. Upstairs is a guest room, a children's den area, two family bedrooms, and the master suite. Look for the cozy fireplace, tray ceiling, and sumptuous bath in the master suite.

plan # HPK0800081

Style: Georgian
First Floor: 1,053 sq. ft.
Second Floor: 1,053 sq. ft.
Total: 2,106 sq. ft.
Bonus Space: 212 sq. ft.
Bedrooms: 4
Bathrooms: 3
Width: 54' - 4"
Depth: 34' - 0"
Foundation: Walkout Basement

SEARCH ONLINE @ EPLANS.COM

QUOTE ONE®

SECOND FLOOR

Brick takes a bold stand with grand traditional style in this treasured design. From the front entry to the rear deck, the floor plan serves family needs in just over 2,000 square feet. The front study has a nearby full bath, making it a handy guest bedroom. The family room with a fireplace opens to a cozy breakfast area. For more formal entertaining, there's a dining room just off the entry. Upstairs, the master bedroom offers a sitting room and a walk-in closet.

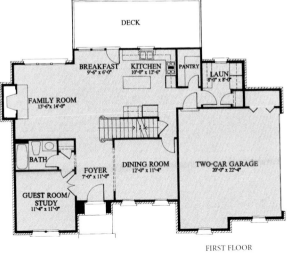

FIRST FLOOR

This Southern Colonial beauty will be the showpiece of any neighborhood, with prominent columns, multipane window dormers, and flower-box accents. Inside, it is instantly clear that this luxurious home is designed with your ultimate comfort in mind. Columns define the dining room from the raised-ceiling foyer; both the dining room and nearby guest suite have French-door access to the front porch. The vaulted great room makes an elegant statement with a bookshelf-framed fireplace and rear French doors topped by a radius window. The island kitchen is definitely made for gourmet entertaining, complete with a butler's pantry and a serving bar to the bayed breakfast nook. The adjacent vaulted keeping room is perfect for cozy gatherings. The left wing is devoted to the master suite, decadent with a sitting bay and a vaulted bath with a step-up tub. Expansion options include a fifth bedroom and full bath.

plan# HPK0800082

Style: Georgian
Square Footage: 3,190
Bonus Space: 305 sq. ft.
Bedrooms: 4
Bathrooms: 3½
Width: 74' - 0"
Depth: 84' - 6"
Foundation: Crawlspace, Basement

SEARCH ONLINE @ EPLANS.COM

© Stephen Fuller, Inc.

This home features keystone arches that frame the arched front door and windows. Inside, the foyer opens directly to the large great room with a fireplace and French doors that lead outside. Just off the foyer, the dining room is defined by columns. Adjacent to the breakfast room is the keeping room, which includes a corner fireplace and more French doors to the large rear porch. The master suite has dual vanities and a spacious walk-in closet. Upstairs, two family bedrooms enjoy separate access to a shared bath; down the hall, a fourth bedroom includes a private bath.

SECOND FLOOR

FIRST FLOOR

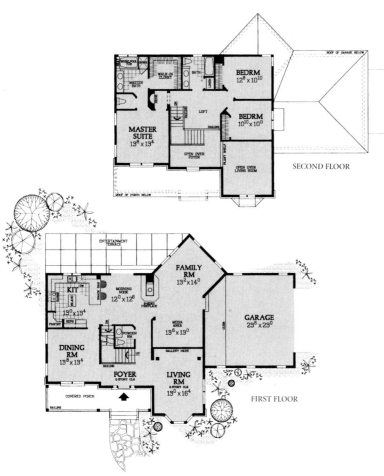

SECOND FLOOR

FIRST FLOOR

plan# HPK0800084

Style: Georgian
First Floor: 1,447 sq. ft.
Second Floor: 958 sq. ft.
Total: 2,405 sq. ft.
Bedrooms: 3
Bathrooms: 2½
Width: 66' - 4"
Depth: 48' - 0"
Foundation: Basement

SEARCH ONLINE @ EPLANS.COM

The asymmetrical front facade of this three-bedroom, traditional-style home offers great curb appeal. The two-story foyer provides access to all rooms, including the formal living room and dining room. The large U-shaped kitchen features a walk-in pantry, an island, and a snack bar linked to the morning nook with its terrace access. The family room is complete with a three-sided fireplace. Upstairs, the master suite features a large bath with a walk-in closet and a special whirlpool tub with a seat. Two family bedrooms share a full hall bath and a multimedia loft.

NORTHERN COLONIALS

Colonial homes remain the most common building form in New England, for both old and new homes, from villages to remote farms.

Northern Colonials follow many of the same styles as their Southern counterparts, but with some significant differences—beginning with building products. Wood was plentiful in the Northern colonies, so wood-frame walls would be covered by clapboards or shingles.

Steeply pitched roofs kept snow from piling up atop Northern homes, typically with a massive chimney at the center to warm the small, low-ceilinged rooms inside. Windows were small and shuttered to keep out drafts—another element that has changed over the years thanks to more energy-efficient glass, allowing modern homes to enjoy views and natural light.

A little south of New England, in the Dutch Colonial regions of New York and New Jersey, one- or one-and-a-half story homes dominated, often topped by a gently sloping roof.

Many early Colonial homes had a lean-to added to the back of the house for additional storage or living space. This evolved into the steep, long back roof of the saltbox style, which provided added space on the first floor. ∎

Design HPK0800107 (page 110) incorporates architectural elements from early Colonial homes, like the Georgian-inspired entryway, with the farmhouse style that gained popularity in the 19th Century.

Brick and shake create a weathered look for this Colonial home, complemented by a pediment entry; use recycled materials for a more vintage appeal. A two-story foyer is graced with French doors to the living room/study. A two-story family room is enhanced by radius windows and a warming fireplace. The serving-bar kitchen is conveniently central to the bayed breakfast nook and formal dining room. Upstairs, three family bedrooms (one lit by dormer windows) share a full bath. The master suite resides in luxury with a sumptuous private bath that includes a vaulted ceiling and corner tub.

plan# HPK0800085

Style: NE Colonial
First Floor: 1,186 sq. ft.
Second Floor: 1,210 sq. ft.
Total: 2,396 sq. ft.
Bedrooms: 4
Bathrooms: 2½
Width: 50' - 0"
Depth: 47' - 6"
Foundation: Crawlspace, Basement

SEARCH ONLINE @ EPLANS.COM

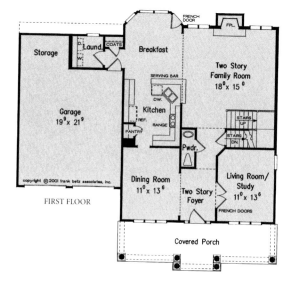

FIRST FLOOR

SECOND FLOOR

plan# HPK0800086

Style: NE Colonial
First Floor: 1,736 sq. ft.
Second Floor: 1,650 sq. ft.
Total: 3,386 sq. ft.
Bedrooms: 5
Bathrooms: 4½
Width: 62' - 0"
Depth: 56' - 0"
Foundation: Crawlspace, Basement

SEARCH ONLINE @ EPLANS.COM

This spirited Early American design employs brick and siding for classic good looks and timeless appeal. A pediment-style entry opens to the foyer, lit by an arched second-story window. On the right, columns define the formal dining room. Continue to the two-story family room, where a rear bowed window wall makes a grand impression and affords stunning views. A well-planned kitchen is designed for entertaining, with stacked dual ovens, miles of counter space, and a serving bar that overlooks the bayed breakfast nook and hearth-warmed keeping room. A guest suite is tucked to the far left for privacy. Upstairs, secondary bedrooms are well appointed. The master suite dazzles with a sitting room, vast walk-in closets, and a vaulted bath with a spa tub. A laundry room on this level is the ultimate convenience.

FIRST FLOOR

SECOND FLOOR

SECOND FLOOR

FIRST FLOOR

plan# HPK0800087

Style: Georgian
First Floor: 1,661 sq. ft.
Second Floor: 1,600 sq. ft.
Total: 3,261 sq. ft.
Bedrooms: 5
Bathrooms: 4
Width: 56' - 0"
Depth: 48' - 0"
Foundation: Crawlspace, Basement

SEARCH ONLINE @ EPLANS.COM

This handsome Georgian Colonial combines the classic look of siding with stately brick for an unforgettable home. From the covered entry, the two-story foyer opens to formal rooms at either side. An overlook from above defines the two-story family room, emphasized by tall radius windows. A fireplace here can be viewed from the angled kitchen and bayed breakfast nook. The guest room is designed for privacy. Three upper-level bedrooms (one with a private bath) are full of natural light. The master suite invokes a unique spirit with a bayed sitting area, private porch, and exquisite bath.

ORDER BLUEPRINTS 24 HOURS, 7 DAYS A WEEK, AT 1-800-521-6797

plan# HPK0800088

Style: Northern Colonial
First Floor: 1,381 sq. ft.
Second Floor: 1,644 sq. ft.
Total: 3,025 sq. ft.
Bedrooms: 5
Bathrooms: 3
Width: 53' - 10"
Depth: 41' - 6"
Foundation: Crawlspace, Basement

SEARCH ONLINE @ EPLANS.COM

Subtle brick accents lend distinctive character to this Cape Cod beauty. Enter to a two-story foyer; a private study with French doors is to the right. On the left, a formal dining room is designed for entertaining. The gourmet kitchen features an island and a serving bar for easy meal preparation. Near the sunny breakfast bay, a bedroom with a full bath makes an ideal guest room. Relax in the family room full of natural light and warmed by a cozy fireplace. Upstairs, the master suite reigns with a vaulted bath and the option to expand into Bedroom 4. Two additional bedrooms share a full bath and a children's retreat.

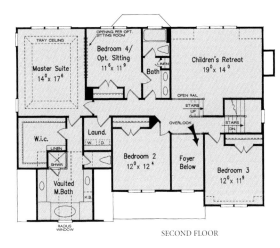

SECOND FLOOR

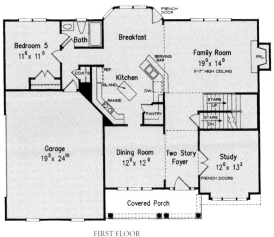

FIRST FLOOR

Colonial splendor is at hand in this stately Early American design. Two entries include a central pediment and a side covered porch; inside, formal spaces are to the front of the home. The dining room connects to the show-stopping kitchen through a butler's pantry. Here, a prominent island joins dual ovens and a bayed sink counter to regale chefs and guests alike. The bayed breakfast nook is perfect for casual meals; the adjacent hearth-warmed family room invites relaxation. Upstairs, secondary bedrooms are generously appointed, but the real star is the opulent master suite. An optional corner fireplace adds to the decadent ambiance; an arch leads to the private sitting room. A trayed-ceiling bath hosts a spa tub and seated shower. The walk-in closet accommodates an impressive wardrobe with storage space to spare.

plan# HPK0800089

Style: Colonial
First Floor: 1,526 sq. ft.
Second Floor: 1,805 sq. ft.
Total: 3,331 sq. ft.
Bedrooms: 4
Bathrooms: 3½
Width: 63' - 0"
Depth: 44' - 0"
Foundation: Crawlspace, Basement

SEARCH ONLINE @ EPLANS.COM

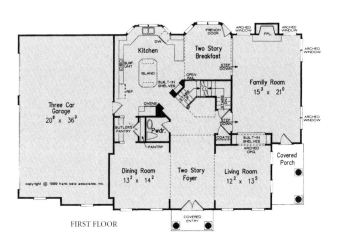

FIRST FLOOR

SECOND FLOOR

ORDER BLUEPRINTS 24 HOURS, 7 DAYS A WEEK, AT 1-800-521-6797

plan# HPK0800090

Style: NE Colonial
First Floor: 2,101 sq. ft.
Second Floor: 1,127 sq. ft.
Total: 3,228 sq. ft.
Bedrooms: 5
Bathrooms: 3½
Width: 58' - 4"
Depth: 58' - 0"
Foundation: Basement

SEARCH ONLINE @ EPLANS.COM

In your neighborhood, this upscale Colonial house will receive many accolades. Its attention-grabbing gables and hipped rooflines, along with shuttered windows and a brick facade, say it all. Visitors will enter the two-story foyer through an elegant covered porch or directly into the dining room through French doors. Toward the back, the two-story grand room has a multiwindowed bay facing the outside deck. The morning and keeping rooms open to the deck through French doors and provide enough natural light to warm all family members. On the right side of the plan, a plush master suite offers a six-sided sitting room with a bay window. Four bedrooms share two baths on the second level, and there's also room to develop additional space. The plan comes with a 2,000-square-foot finished basement.

SECOND FLOOR

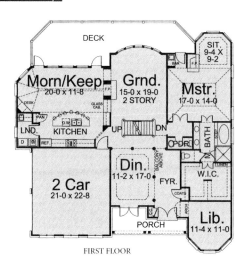

FIRST FLOOR

This grand house, with shuttered windows, majestic columns, gables, and hipped rooflines, is the best of what Early American style offers. Designed for genteel entertaining, as well as comfy family get-togethers, you'll find all your needs met here. A spacious kitchen flows into a uniquely shaped morning room flooded with natural light, and an old-fashioned keeping room. Here's where family members will be found sipping an eye-opening cup of coffee or dipping into a late-night bowl of ice cream. The dining area and a grand room with a fireplace run into each other, amplifying the sense of space. An opulent master suite with an adjoining study makes up the entire left side of the first level. Upstairs, three bedrooms, two baths, and space for another bedroom, study, or game room are located.

plan# HPK0800091

Style: NE Colonial
First Floor: 2,253 sq. ft.
Second Floor: 1,002 sq. ft.
Total: 3,255 sq. ft.
Bedrooms: 4
Bathrooms: 3½
Width: 61' - 6"
Depth: 64' - 0"
Foundation: Basement

SEARCH ONLINE @ EPLANS.COM

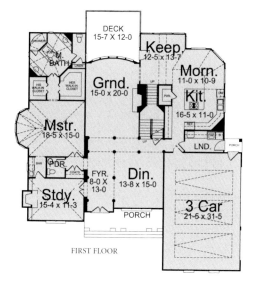

FIRST FLOOR

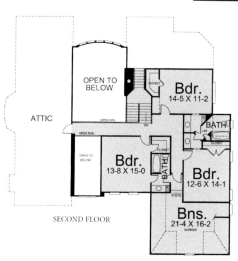

SECOND FLOOR

plan# HPK0800092

Style: NE Colonial
First Floor: 1,904 sq. ft.
Second Floor: 869 sq. ft.
Total: 2,773 sq. ft.
Bedrooms: 4
Bathrooms: 3½
Width: 60' - 0"
Depth: 54' - 0"
Foundation: Basement

SEARCH ONLINE @ EPLANS.COM

SECOND FLOOR

This classic Early American home will dress up your neighborhood and give your family a congenial environment to grow and develop. Four bedrooms, including a master suite with a wonderfully equipped bath aimed at soothing relaxation, provide ample sleeping quarters. The master bedroom has entry to the rear deck. The kitchen is designed to easily serve the family room and breakfast nook; the living room boasts a warming fireplace. A substantial storage area has been placed on the second level with three family bedrooms. The laundry opens to a small side deck and to the two-car garage.

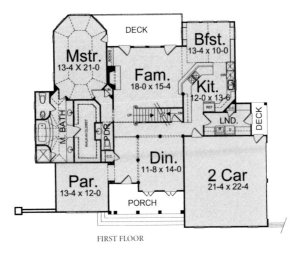

FIRST FLOOR

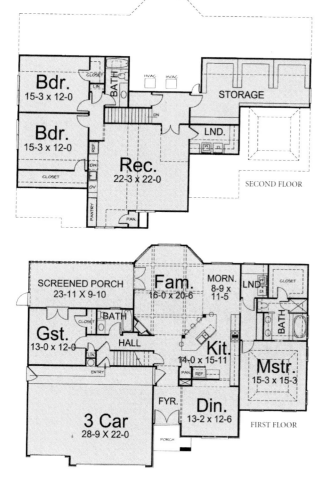

Bdr.
15-3 x 12-0

Bdr.
15-3 x 12-0

BATH

STORAGE

LND.

Rec.
22-3 x 22-0

SECOND FLOOR

SCREENED PORCH
23-11 X 9-10

Fam.
16-0 x 20-6

MORN.
8-9 x
11-5

LND

BATH

Gst.
13-0 x 12-0

HALL

Kit.
14-0 x 15-11

Mstr.
15-3 x 15-3

ENTRY

3 Car
28-9 X 22-0

FYR.

Din.
13-2 x 12-6

FIRST FLOOR

PORCH

plan# HPK0800093

Style: NE Colonial
First Floor: 1,758 sq. ft.
Second Floor: 1,087 sq. ft.
Total: 2,845 sq. ft.
Bonus Space: 307 sq. ft.
Bedrooms: 2
Bathrooms: 3
Width: 65' - 0"
Depth: 49' - 9"
Foundation: Slab

SEARCH ONLINE @ EPLANS.COM

Charming Colonial and European accents grace the exterior of this quaint design. Inside, the foyer is flanked on either side by a formal dining room and a study that easily converts to a guest bedroom. Straight ahead, the family room warmed by a fireplace accesses the rear screened porch. The snack-bar kitchen overlooks the casual morning room and family room. The first-floor master suite features a private bath and a walk-in closet. This floor is completed by a three-car garage and a laundry room. Upstairs, an additional bedroom provides a walk-in closet and a hall bath is conveniently close. The recreation room is great for entertaining family or friends. A second-floor laundry is placed just across from the office, which accesses the attic space.

With all the quaint character of the New England coast, this remarkable Colonial design features all the drama of the past with the all the amenities of the future. A portico welcomes you inside to a foyer flanked on either side by a parlor and formal dining room. The two-story grand room and keeping room share a see-through fireplace. The snack-bar kitchen offers a casual morning room nearby. The laundry room connects to the three-car garage. On the opposite side of the home, the first-floor master suite provides a private bath and double walk-in closet. A breathtaking staircase curves to the second floor from the foyer. Three additional bedrooms are available on the second floor, along with optional attic space.

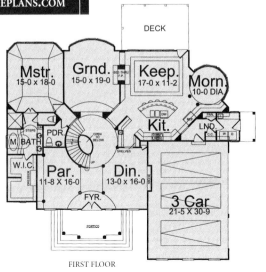

FIRST FLOOR

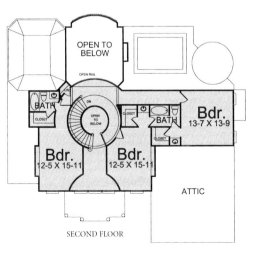

SECOND FLOOR

This Northeastern Colonial design features an impressive family-oriented layout. The front porch welcomes you inside to a foyer flanked on either side by a formal dining room and a library warmed by a fireplace. Past the cascading staircase, the grand room is enhanced by a fireplace with flanking built-ins. From here, double doors open to a rear veranda. A fireplace warms the combined keeping and morning room, which connects to the kitchen. The first-floor master suite provides private access to the veranda, a pampering bath, and walk-in closet. Four additional bedrooms are located on the second floor. An optional apartment is available above the three-car garage.

plan# HPK0800095

Style: NE Colonial
First Floor: 2,295 sq. ft.
Second Floor: 1,106 sq. ft.
Total: 3,401 sq. ft.
Bedrooms: 5
Bathrooms: 3½
Width: 52' - 0"
Depth: 84' - 0"
Foundation: Crawlspace

SEARCH ONLINE @ EPLANS.COM

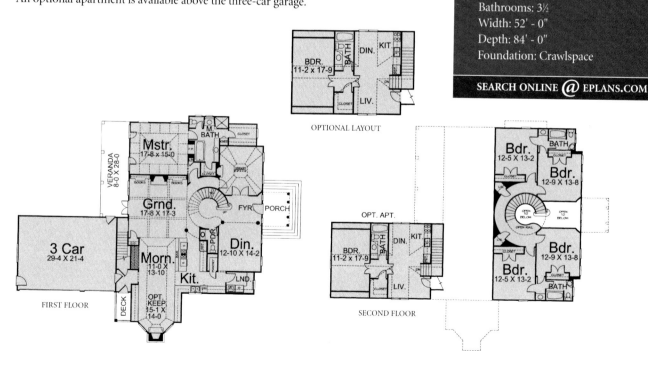

OPTIONAL LAYOUT

FIRST FLOOR

SECOND FLOOR

ORDER BLUEPRINTS 24 HOURS, 7 DAYS A WEEK, AT 1-800-521-6797

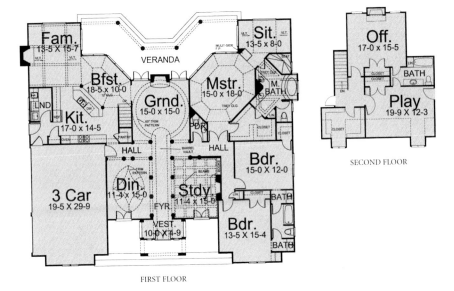

plan # HPK0800096

Style: NE Colonial
First Floor: 2,834 sq. ft.
Second Floor: 778 sq. ft.
Total: 3,612 sq. ft.
Bedrooms: 4
Bathrooms: 3½
Width: 80' - 6"
Depth: 70' - 8"
Foundation: Slab,
Crawlspace, Basement

SEARCH ONLINE @ EPLANS.COM

The facade of this Colonial home offers classical accents and striking symmetry. A vestibule welcomes you inside to a foyer flanked by an impressive study and a formal dining room. Straight ahead, the grand room is warmed by a fireplace and provides double sets of French doors accessing the rear veranda. The left side of the home is a casual gathering area for the family, which includes a snack-bar kitchen, a breakfast room, and the family room warmed by another fireplace. A laundry room and three-car garage are easily accessed from the kitchen. Family sleeping quarters reside to the right of the plan. The master suite is pampering with a double walk-in closet, master bath, and sitting room. Two additional family bedrooms share a Jack-and-Jill bath. A home office with a third fireplace, a playroom, a full bath, and walk-in closet storage reside upstairs.

SECOND FLOOR

FIRST FLOOR

Dormers and transom windows lend charm to this Colonial design. Inside, columns define the formal dining room to the right of the foyer, and the study to the left of the foyer is accessed by double doors. The vaulted family room offers a corner fireplace. A bay window, large closet, and spacious private bath highlight the first-floor master suite; a bay window also decorates the breakfast area. Upstairs are three family bedrooms, all with walk-in closets, and two full baths.

plan# HPK0800097

Style: NE Colonial
First Floor: 1,907 sq. ft.
Second Floor: 908 sq. ft.
Total: 2,815 sq. ft.
Bonus Space: 183 sq. ft.
Bedrooms: 4
Bathrooms: 3½
Width: 64' - 8"
Depth: 51' - 0"

SEARCH ONLINE @ EPLANS.COM

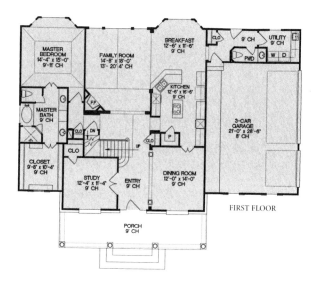

FIRST FLOOR

SECOND FLOOR

ORDER BLUEPRINTS 24 HOURS, 7 DAYS A WEEK, AT 1-800-521-6797

plan# HPK0800098

Style: NE Colonial
First Floor: 802 sq. ft.
Second Floor: 757 sq. ft.
Total: 1,559 sq. ft.
Bedrooms: 3
Bathrooms: 2½
Width: 47' - 0"
Depth: 38' - 6"
Foundation: Basement

SEARCH ONLINE @ EPLANS.COM

Offering a smaller space while still providing today's necessary amenities, this two-story traditional home would be ideal for smaller or corner lots. Inside, the foyer leads to all the living areas available on the first floor. The combination living and dining room features a large fireplace and access to the rear patio. The corner kitchen includes plenty of counter space and a pass-through to the breakfast nook with a sunny bay window. Upstairs, two family bedrooms share a full hall bath, while the master bedroom features its own bath with dual sinks. A large storage area on the second floor and a half-bath on the first floor complete this versatile plan.

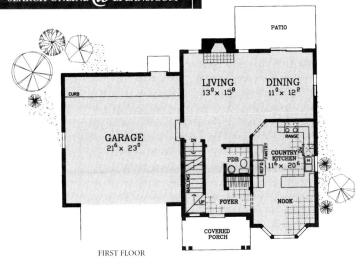

FIRST FLOOR

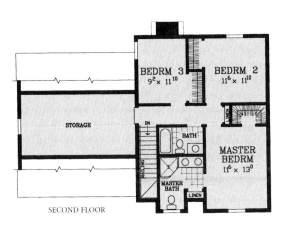

SECOND FLOOR

This attractive multilevel home is rich with exterior detail and offers early-century charm coupled with modern amenities. Formal and informal spaces are provided, with the open hearth room, kitchen, and breakfast area serving as an exciting gathering place for family members. The first-floor mudroom or laundry provides a buffer to the garage and outdoors. Split stairs, graced with wood banisters, lead to the second floor. The lavish master bedroom is topped with a tray ceiling and offers a deluxe bath and a large walk-in closet. A front bedroom can be converted to an open loft overlooking the stairway. Continuing to the third floor, a bonus room provides optional space and a full bath allows this to be a private bedroom retreat.

plan# HPK0800099

Style: Colonial
First Floor: 1,074 sq. ft.
Second Floor: 884 sq. ft.
Total: 1,958 sq. ft.
Bonus Space: 299 sq. ft.
Bedrooms: 3
Bathrooms: 3½
Width: 50' - 10"
Depth: 47' - 0"
Foundation: Basement

SEARCH ONLINE @ EPLANS.COM

FIRST FLOOR

SECOND FLOOR

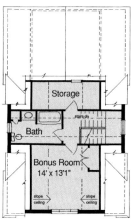

OPTIONAL LAYOUT

plan # HPK0800100

Style: NE Colonial
First Floor: 886 sq. ft.
Second Floor: 868 sq. ft.
Total: 1,754 sq. ft.
Bedrooms: 3
Bathrooms: 1½
Width: 32' - 0"
Depth: 28' - 0"
Foundation: Basement

SEARCH ONLINE @ EPLANS.COM

Inside this lovely New England Colonial home, the foyer is flanked by a living room and cozy den. The kitchen features a snack bar and dining area. A utility room completes the first floor. Upstairs, three family bedrooms share a whirlpool bath. A bonus room—perfect for a guest suite or home office—is located above the detached garage.

FIRST FLOOR

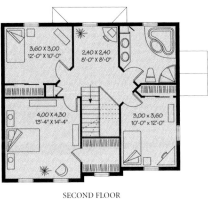

SECOND FLOOR

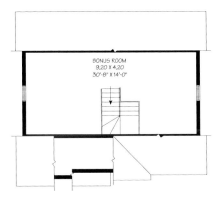

Full of tradition and sensibility, this classic design will be joy to call home for generations to come. Living areas are ready for busy family life and invite relaxation with spacious rooms and lots of natural light. Casual and formal dining areas are convenient to the open kitchen. A U-shaped staircase leads up to three bedrooms, including an engaging master suite with a corner spa tub and plenty of storage. A one-car garage completes this home perfectly.

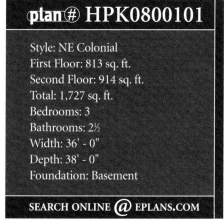

plan# HPK0800101

Style: NE Colonial
First Floor: 813 sq. ft.
Second Floor: 914 sq. ft.
Total: 1,727 sq. ft.
Bedrooms: 3
Bathrooms: 2½
Width: 36' - 0"
Depth: 38' - 0"
Foundation: Basement

SEARCH ONLINE @ EPLANS.COM

FIRST FLOOR

SECOND FLOOR

plan# HPK0800102

Style: NE Colonial
First Floor: 804 sq. ft.
Second Floor: 918 sq. ft.
Total: 1,722 sq. ft.
Bedrooms: 3
Bathrooms: 2½
Width: 36' - 0"
Depth: 38' - 0"
Foundation: Basement

SEARCH ONLINE @ EPLANS.COM

This beautiful Colonial-style home features incredible living spaces in less than 2,000 square feet. A detailed porch entry opens to the mudroom/foyer, designed for winter chill with a secondary "airlock" door. The family gathering room warms and welcomes with a cozy two-sided fireplace, shared with the dining area. The kitchen hosts an island snack bar and is conveniently situated near the walk-in pantry, laundry room, and half-bath. Bedrooms are all located on the second floor. The master suite is a resplendent retreat with a private whirlpool bath and walk-in closet. Two additional bedrooms share a bath to complete the plan.

SECOND FLOOR

FIRST FLOOR

This two-story design faithfully recalls the 18th-Century homestead of Secretary of Foreign Affairs John Jay. First-floor livability includes a grand living room with a fireplace and a music alcove. The nearby library also sports a fireplace and convenient built-ins. A large country kitchen delights with another fireplace and a snack bar. A large clutter room has an attached half-bath and allows plenty of space for hobbies or a workshop. Three upstairs bedrooms include a large master suite with a walk-in closet, vanity seating, and double sinks. Each family bedroom contains a double closet.

plan # HPK0800103

Style: NE Colonial
First Floor: 2,026 sq. ft.
Second Floor: 1,386 sq. ft.
Total: 3,412 sq. ft.
Bedrooms: 3
Bathrooms: 2½ + ½
Width: 84' - 0"
Depth: 65' - 8"
Foundation: Basement

SEARCH ONLINE @ EPLANS.COM

QUOTE ONE®

FIRST FLOOR

SECOND FLOOR

ORDER BLUEPRINTS 24 HOURS, 7 DAYS A WEEK, AT 1-800-521-6797

MILES MELTON
CARY, NC

plan# HPK0800104

Style: Colonial
First Floor: 2,273 sq. ft.
Second Floor: 1,391 sq. ft.
Total: 3,664 sq. ft.
Bonus Space: 547 sq. ft.
Bedrooms: 4
Bathrooms: 4½
Width: 77' - 2"
Depth: 48' - 0"
Foundation: Crawlspace

SEARCH ONLINE @ EPLANS.COM

An easy and charming interpretation of the Late Georgian style, this plan is carefully adapted to meet the practical requirements of a modern lifestyle. Cased openings, high ceilings, and well-placed windows keep the expansive, comfortable interiors well-lighted and open. The spacious family room, which enjoys a fireplace flanked by built-in shelves, opens to the rear terrace. The lavish master suite enjoys privacy on the first level; the other three bedrooms—each with private baths—are comfortably situated on the second floor. Additional space is available upstairs to develop a recreation room.

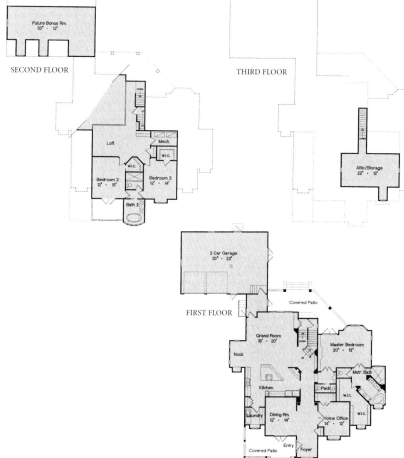

SECOND FLOOR

Future Bonus Rm.
33" · 12"

Loft

Mech.

w.i.c.

w.i.c.

Bedroom 2
12" · 15"

Bedroom 3
12" · 14"

Bath 2

THIRD FLOOR

Attic/Storage
22" · 12"

FIRST FLOOR

2 Car Garage
33" · 22"

Covered Patio

Grand Room
19' · 20'

Nook

Master Bedroom
20" · 13'

Mstr. Bath

Kitchen

Pwdr.

w.i.c.

Laundry

Dining Rm.
12" · 14"

Home Office
14" · 12"

w.i.c.

Covered Patio

Entry

Foyer

plan# HPK0800105

Style: NE Colonial
First Floor: 2,376 sq. ft.
Second Floor: 1,078 sq. ft.
Total: 3,454 sq. ft.
Bonus Space: 549 sq. ft.
Bedrooms: 3
Bathrooms: 2½
Width: 80' - 6"
Depth: 85' - 6"
Foundation: Slab

SEARCH ONLINE @ EPLANS.COM

An abundance of muntin windows

and a shingle facade are the defining characteristics
of this design. Inside, the dining room is graced with
French doors to the covered front porch. A home
office flanks the foyer on the right. The master bedroom boasts a full bath, His and Hers walk-in closets,
and French-door access to the rear covered porch.
The grand room flows into the nook and kitchen.
The second level holds two family bedrooms that
share a lavish walk-through bath. A large future
bonus room and a loft complete this level. The third
floor houses a spacious attic/storage room.

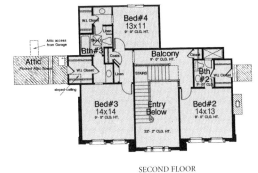

plan # HPK0800106

Style: NE Colonial
First Floor: 2,814 sq. ft.
Second Floor: 979 sq. ft.
Total: 3,793 sq. ft.
Bedrooms: 4
Bathrooms: 3½
Width: 98' - 0"
Depth: 45' - 10"
Foundation: Slab,
Basement, Crawlspace

SEARCH ONLINE @ EPLANS.COM

SECOND FLOOR

FIRST FLOOR

On the exterior, decorative quoins and keystone moldings match the elegance of the columned entryway and bring an irresistible Colonial flair to the design. The layout is equally American, though modern: island kitchen with adjoining dining room and breakfast nook, and easy movement into the magnificent family room, with fireplace and cathedral ceiling. A gallery provides a transition to the right wing of the home, dominated by the study, master suite, and luxury bath. Separation from the public spaces of the home ensures quiet enjoyment for the homeowners. On the second floor, three bedrooms share two baths. The balcony overlooks an impressive foyer.

With five bedrooms and a wonderful stone-and-siding exterior, this country home will satisfy every need. Two sets of French doors provide access to the dining room and foyer. The great room enjoys a warming fireplace and deck access. The kitchen, breakfast bay, and keeping room feature an open floor plan. A charming sitting area in a bay window sets off the master bedroom. The master bath features a large walk-in closet, two-sink vanity, separate tub and shower, and compartmented toilet. Four bedrooms, an office, and two full baths complete the upper level.

REAR EXTERIOR

plan # HPK0800107

Style: NE Colonial
First Floor: 2,628 sq. ft.
Second Floor: 1,775 sq. ft.
Total: 4,403 sq. ft.
Bedrooms: 5
Bathrooms: 3½
Width: 79' - 6"
Depth: 65' - 1"
Foundation: Walkout Basement

SEARCH ONLINE @ EPLANS.COM

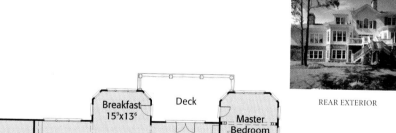

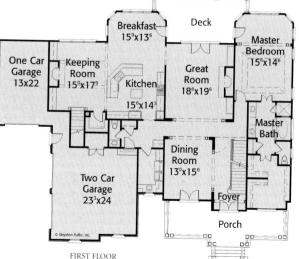

FIRST FLOOR

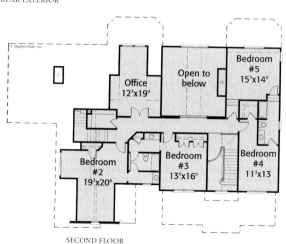

SECOND FLOOR

SOUTHERN COLONIALS

Soil rich with clay made brick production relatively easy in the South, and bricks quickly became the building material of choice for Southern Colonial homes. The bright colors and rich textures of brick lent a unique charm to the sharp lines of Colonial architecture.

Other regional nuances included larger windows than those in Northern homes. These could open and bring a breeze through the house to combat the hot Southern summers. Later, Southern homes would be the first to add porches, since they could protect parts of the first floor from direct sunlight.

Paired chimneys at either end of the home were more common in the South than the North, as were gently sloping roofs, without the threat of snow. Hipped roofs were also more common in the South, as opposed to the side-gabled or gambrel styles in the North.

Large Early Classic Revival homes can be found in the Southern colonies as well, featuring a gabled, full-height front porch supported by columns and a front door typically topped with an arched window. These homes, appearing in the late 18th Century, were a precursor to the Greek Revival homes that became popular nationwide shortly thereafter.■

The full-height, full-width front porch on Design HPK0800109 (page 113) was characteristic of many Southern Colonial homes.

Southern grandeur is evident in this wonderful two-story design with its magnificent second-floor balcony. The formal living spaces—dining room and living room—flank the impressive foyer with its stunning staircase. The family room resides in the rear, opening to the terrace. The sunny breakfast bay adjoins the island kitchen for efficient planning. The right wing holds the two-car garage, utility room, a secondary staircase, and a study that can easily be converted to a guest suite with a private bath. The master suite and Bedrooms 2 and 3 are placed on the second floor.

plan# HPK0800108

Style: Southern Colonial
First Floor: 2,033 sq. ft.
Second Floor: 1,447 sq. ft.
Total: 3,480 sq. ft.
Bonus Space: 411 sq. ft.
Bedrooms: 3
Bathrooms: 3½
Width: 67' - 10"
Depth: 64' - 4"
Foundation: Crawlspace, Basement

SEARCH ONLINE @ EPLANS.COM

ORDER BLUEPRINTS 24 HOURS, 7 DAYS A WEEK, AT 1-800-521-6797

plan# HPK0800109

Style: Southern Colonial
First Floor: 1,273 sq. ft.
Second Floor: 1,358 sq. ft.
Total: 2,631 sq. ft.
Bedrooms: 4
Bathrooms: 3½
Width: 54' - 10"
Depth: 48' - 6"
Foundation: Crawlspace

SEARCH ONLINE @ EPLANS.COM

This two-story home suits the needs of each household member. Family gatherings won't be crowded in the spacious family room, which is adjacent to the kitchen and the breakfast area. Just beyond the foyer, the dining and living rooms view the front yard. The master suite features its own full bath with dual vanities, a whirlpool tub, and separate shower. Three family bedrooms—one with a walk-in closet—and two full hall baths are available upstairs. Extra storage space is found in the two-car garage.

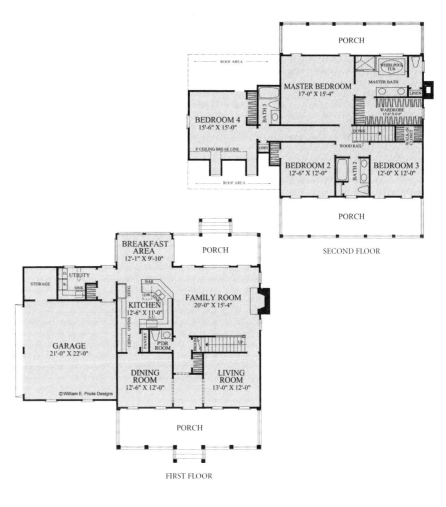

SECOND FLOOR

FIRST FLOOR

© The Sater Design Collection, Inc.

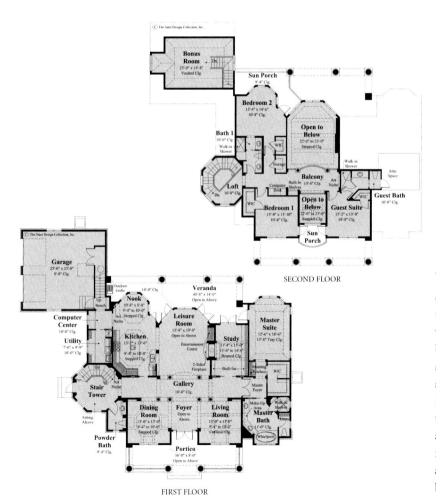

SECOND FLOOR

FIRST FLOOR

This appealing French Country design emphasizes effective indoor/outdoor relationships. A wide, welcoming front porch can be viewed from the living and dining rooms; to the back of the plan, the kitchen, leisure room, and study all open to the lanai. Upstairs, Bedroom 1 shares a balcony with the guest suite, while Bedroom 2 opens to a private deck. Other amenities include a fireplace shared by the living room and study, stepped ceilings in the living and dining rooms, kitchen, and study, and plenty of counter and cabinet space in the utility room. A vaulted bonus room above the garage offers room to grow.

SECOND FLOOR

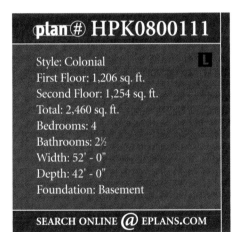

plan # HPK0800111

L

Style: Colonial
First Floor: 1,206 sq. ft.
Second Floor: 1,254 sq. ft.
Total: 2,460 sq. ft.
Bedrooms: 4
Bathrooms: 2½
Width: 52' - 0"
Depth: 42' - 0"
Foundation: Basement

SEARCH ONLINE @ EPLANS.COM

QUOTE ONE®

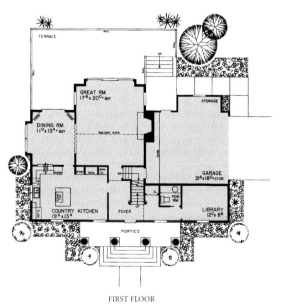

FIRST FLOOR

Clapboards, a center entrance, and symmetrically placed shuttered windows give a distinctly Georgian ambiance, until a Greek Revival portico with four soaring columns and a pediment is added. Inside, a library offers a quiet retreat to the right of the foyer. To the left, the country kitchen provides plenty of room for a table, an island cooktop, and a pass-through to the dining room. Between the pantry and the broom closet sits a built-in desk. The great room is outstanding, with a high ceiling, a wall of windows, and a fireplace. Upstairs, the master suite includes a balcony overlooking the foyer and a bath with twin vanities. Laundry facilities are on this floor, as are a lounge and three family bedrooms sharing a full bath.

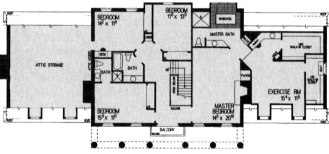

SECOND FLOOR

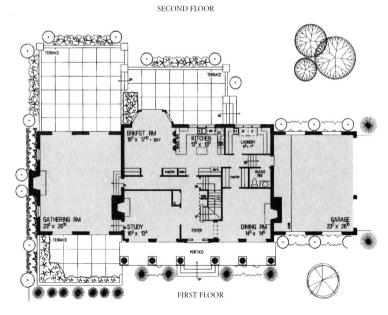

FIRST FLOOR

The elegant facade of this design, with its columned portico, fanlights, and dormers, houses an amenity-filled interior. The gathering room, study, and dining room, each with a fireplace, provide plenty of room for relaxing and entertaining. A large work area contains a kitchen with a breakfast room, a snack bar, a laundry room, and a pantry. The four-bedroom second floor includes a master suite with a sumptuous private bath and an exercise room. Attic storage is available above the gathering room.

QUOTE ONE®

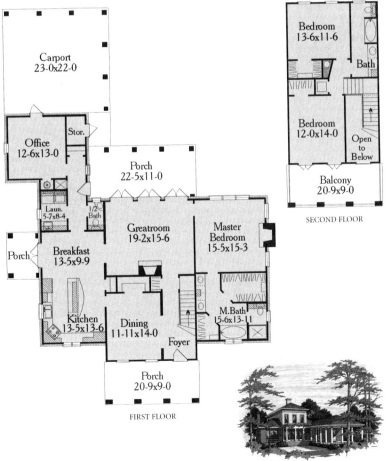

FIRST FLOOR

Carport
23-0x22-0

Office
12-6x13-0

Stor.

Laun.
5-7x8-4

1/2
Bath

Porch

Breakfast
13-5x9-9

Porch
22-5x11-0

Greatroom
19-2x15-6

Master
Bedroom
15-5x15-3

Kitchen
13-5x13-6

Dining
11-11x14-0

Foyer

M.Bath
15-6x13-11

Porch
20-9x9-0

SECOND FLOOR

Bedroom
13-6x11-6

Bath

Bedroom
12-0x14-0

Open
to
Below

Balcony
20-9x9-0

Straight from the South, this home sets a country tone. This Southern Colonial design boasts decorative two-story columns and large windows that enhance the front porch and balcony. Enter through the foyer—notice that the formal dining room on the left connects to the island kitchen. The kitchen opens to a breakfast room, which accesses a side porch that's perfect for outdoor grilling. The great room features a warming fireplace and accesses a rear porch. The master bedroom also includes a fireplace, as well as a private bath with a whirlpool tub and a walk-in closet. A home office, laundry room, and carport complete the first floor. Upstairs, two additional bedrooms share a full hall bath.

REAR EXTERIOR

KEEPING Room Below

RADIUS WINDOW

Vaulted M. Bath

Master Suite
18⁰ x 15⁰

W.i.c

Family Room Below

W.i.c

Bedroom 2
13⁰ x 15⁰

W.i.c

Bath

Bath

Bedroom 3
12⁰ x 12⁵

Foyer Below

Bedroom 4
12⁰ x 12⁵

FRENCH DOOR

FRENCH DOOR

Covered Porch

SECOND FLOOR

Vaulted Keeping Room
13⁵ x 13⁰

Garage
12⁰ x 19⁹

Breakfast

FRENCH DOOR

OVENS

PANTRY

Kitchen

SERVING BAR

Vaulted Family Room
19⁰ x 15⁰

BUILT INS

BUILT INS

Garage
20⁰ x 20³

BUTLERS PANTRY

Laun.

Bath

DECORATIVE COLUMNS

Dining Room
12⁰ x 14⁴

Two Story Foyer

Bedroom 5
12⁰ x 12⁷

Covered Porch

FIRST FLOOR

plan # HPK0800003

Style: Southern Colonial
First Floor: 1,773 sq. ft.
Second Floor: 1,676 sq. ft.
Total: 3,449 sq. ft.
Bedrooms: 5
Bathrooms: 4
Width: 68' - 7"
Depth: 62' - 8"
Foundation: Crawlspace, Basement

SEARCH ONLINE @ EPLANS.COM

From a Colonial past to a contemporary future, this Southern-style home perfectly combines elements of history and modernity. Brick facing graces the entry, where a double-decker porch invites casual relaxation. A two-story foyer opens on the left to an elegant dining room; a butler's pantry makes entertaining simple. The kitchen is a dream come true for the chef who wants room to move and miles of counter space. Adjacent to the bayed breakfast nook, the vaulted keeping room warms with a cozy hearth. The family room completes the living areas with a fireplace and lots of natural light. Upstairs, the master suite is a romantic getaway with a fireplace, room-sized walk-in closet, and a luxuriant vaulted bath.

ORDER BLUEPRINTS 24 HOURS, 7 DAYS A WEEK, AT 1-800-521-6797

plan# HPK0800114

Style: Southern Colonial
First Floor: 2,416 sq. ft.
Second Floor: 1,535 sq. ft.
Total: 3,951 sq. ft.
Bonus Space: 552 sq. ft.
Bedrooms: 5
Bathrooms: 3½
Width: 79' - 2"
Depth: 63' - 6"
Foundation: Crawlspace, Basement

SEARCH ONLINE @ EPLANS.COM

A curved front porch, graceful symmetry in the details, and the sturdiness of brick all combine to enhance this beautiful two-story home. Inside, the two-story foyer introduces the formal rooms—the living room to the right and the dining room to the left—and presents the elegant stairwell. The L-shaped kitchen provides a walk-in pantry, an island with a sink, a butler's pantry, and an adjacent breakfast area. Perfect for casual gatherings, the family room features a fireplace and back-yard access. Located on the first floor for privacy, the master suite offers a large walk-in closet and a lavish bath. Upstairs, four bedrooms—each with a walk-in closet—share two full baths and access to the future recreation room over the garage.

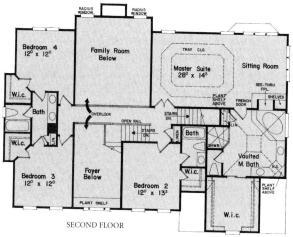

SECOND FLOOR

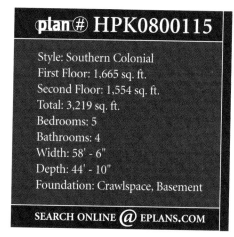

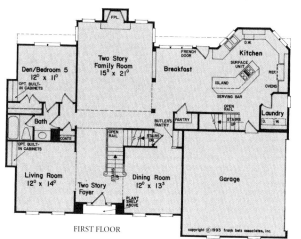

FIRST FLOOR

This stately transitional home focuses on family living. The formal living areas are traditionally placed flanking the two-story foyer. The two-story family room has a lovely fireplace and windows to the rear yard. The remarkable kitchen features wraparound counters, a breakfast nook, and a cooktop island/serving bar. A bedroom and full bath would make a comfortable guest suite or a quiet den. A balcony hall leads to two bedrooms that share a bath; a third bedroom has its own bath and walk-in closet. The master suite is designed with a tray ceiling and a sitting room with a through-fireplace to the vaulted bath.

plan# HPK0800116

Style: Southern Colonial
First Floor: 1,488 sq. ft.
Second Floor: 1,551 sq. ft.
Total: 3,039 sq. ft.
Bedrooms: 5
Bathrooms: 4
Width: 55' - 0"
Depth: 57' - 4"
Foundation: Crawlspace,
Slab, Basement

SEARCH ONLINE @ EPLANS.COM

Traditional lines accentuate the powerful brick facade of this home. Flanked by the formal dining and living rooms, the two-story foyer features a handsome staircase. To the rear of the plan, windows frame the fireplace in the family room, and both the dining room and living room feature tall windows. A guest room is near the full bath on the right of the plan. A roomy island kitchen handles casual to formal meals with ease. On the second floor, the master suite includes a vaulted bath with a radius window over the tub. Three family bedrooms—one with a private bath—complete the living quarters.

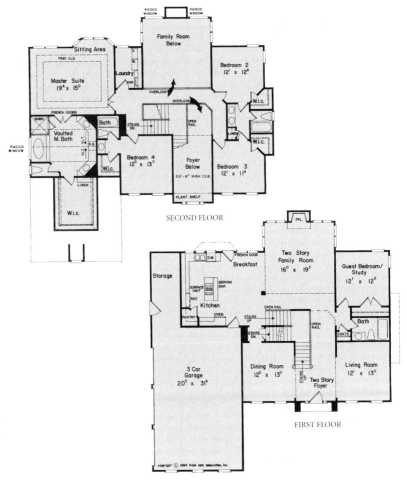

SECOND FLOOR

FIRST FLOOR

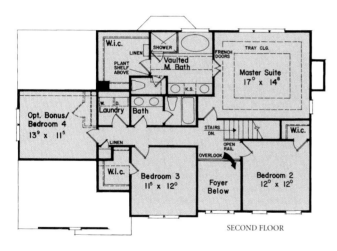

SECOND FLOOR

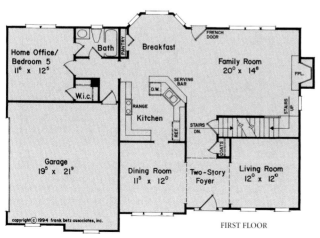

copyright (c) 1994 frank betz associates, inc.

FIRST FLOOR

plan# HPK0800117

Style: Southern Colonial
First Floor: 1,289 sq. ft.
Second Floor: 1,069 sq. ft.
Total: 2,358 sq. ft.
Bonus Space: 168 sq. ft.
Bedrooms: 4
Bathrooms: 3
Width: 54' - 4"
Depth: 37' - 6"
Foundation: Basement, Crawlspace

SEARCH ONLINE @ EPLANS.COM

Traditional stylings—pilaster and sidelight accents at the front entry and keystone jack-arched windows with shutters—present a home with class and appeal. The two-story foyer is flanked by the formal dining room and the living room. Beyond the enclosed staircase, the family room, warmed with a fireplace, offers a cozy environment for intimate gatherings. The angled kitchen enjoys a serving bar and is situated between the dining room and breakfast area for convenience. Note the home office/bedroom, tucked away on the left, with its private entrance to the full bath. The lavish master suite resides on the second floor along with two additional bedrooms, a full bath, laundry, and bonus room.

plan# HPK0800118

Style: Southern Colonial
First Floor: 1,810 sq. ft.
Second Floor: 1,740 sq. ft.
Total: 3,550 sq. ft.
Bedrooms: 5
Bathrooms: 4½
Width: 59' - 0"
Depth: 53' - 0"
Foundation: Crawlspace, Basement

SEARCH ONLINE @ EPLANS.COM

SECOND FLOOR

FIRST FLOOR

Two-story columns and the front bay window with a flared metal hood express the splendor of this stately two-story home. Decorative columns define the family room from the kitchen and breakfast area, and the bedchamber from the sitting room in the master suite. The kitchen—a chef's delight—enjoys loads of counter space, a walk-in pantry, and an island work counter. Front dining and living rooms are designed for refined dinner parties and social gatherings. Upstairs, four bedrooms, including the amenity-filled master suite, open to a balcony overlooking the two-story family room. A fifth bedroom—or make it a study—is located on the main level.

SECOND FLOOR

FIRST FLOOR

copyright © 1998 frank betz associates, inc.

plan⊕ HPK0800119

Style: Southern Colonial
First Floor: 1,463 sq. ft.
Second Floor: 1,490 sq. ft.
Total: 2,953 sq. ft.
Bedrooms: 5
Bathrooms: 4½
Width: 54' - 0"
Depth: 51' - 6"
Foundation: Crawlspace,
Basement, Slab

SEARCH ONLINE @ EPLANS.COM

The nearly octagonal shape of the kitchen, with its long work island, will please the family's gourmet cook. The breakfast room, which opens to the back through a French door, flows into the two-story family room; to one side there's a butler's pantry leading to the dining room. The formal living room is on the other side of the two-story foyer. A bedroom with a private bath and walk-in closet could be an in-law suite, study, or home office. The other four bedrooms are upstairs off a balcony overlooking the family room. The laundry room is also on this floor. The master suite includes a sitting room, a walk-in closet, and a luxurious bath.

ORDER BLUEPRINTS 24 HOURS, 7 DAYS A WEEK, AT 1-800-521-6797

plan # HPK0800120

Style: Southern Colonial
First Floor: 1,415 sq. ft.
Second Floor: 1,632 sq. ft.
Total: 3,047 sq. ft.
Bedrooms: 4
Bathrooms: 3½
Width: 56' - 0"
Depth: 47' - 6"
Foundation: Crawlspace, Basement

SEARCH ONLINE @ EPLANS.COM

This impressive traditional design offers unique room placement to set it apart from other designs. The sun-drenched foyer leads to an angled two-story family room with a corner fireplace, a balcony overlook, and a pass-through to the island kitchen. The kitchen is a dream come true for any gourmand, with amenities that include a walk-in pantry, a writing desk, and plenty of counter space. The bayed breakfast nook, with its French-door access to the rear yard, will be a favorite place to congregate. A formal dining room and a living room with a private covered porch complete the first floor. Upstairs, two bedrooms share a full bath, and Bedroom 4 features its own bath and walk-in closet. The master bedroom suite offers a bayed sitting room—the perfect place to relax—and a master bath with a large walk-in closet.

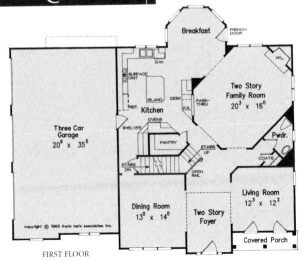

FIRST FLOOR

SECOND FLOOR

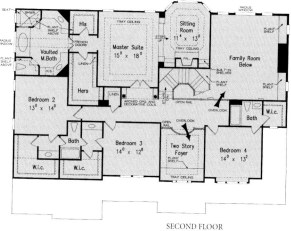

SECOND FLOOR

FIRST FLOOR

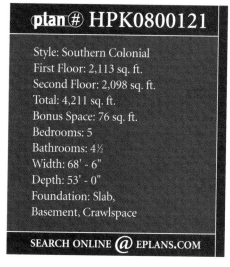

plan # HPK0800121

Style: Southern Colonial
First Floor: 2,113 sq. ft.
Second Floor: 2,098 sq. ft.
Total: 4,211 sq. ft.
Bonus Space: 76 sq. ft.
Bedrooms: 5
Bathrooms: 4½
Width: 68' - 6"
Depth: 53' - 0"
Foundation: Slab,
Basement, Crawlspace

SEARCH ONLINE @ EPLANS.COM

This two-story farmhouse has much to offer, with the most exciting feature being the opulent master suite, which takes up almost the entire width of the upper level. French doors access the large master bedroom with its coffered ceiling. Steps lead to a separate sitting room with a fireplace and sun-filled bay window. His and Hers walk-in closets lead the way to a vaulted private bath with separate vanities and a lavish whirlpool tub. On the first floor, an island kitchen and a bayed breakfast room flow into a two-story family room with a raised-hearth fireplace, built-in shelves, and French-door access to the rear yard.

plan # HPK0800122

Style: Southern Colonial
First Floor: 2,732 sq. ft.
Second Floor: 2,734 sq. ft.
Total: 5,466 sq. ft.
Bedrooms: 5
Bathrooms: 5½ + ½
Width: 85' - 0"
Depth: 85' - 6"
Foundation: Crawlspace,
Slab, Basement

SEARCH ONLINE @ EPLANS.COM

A wraparound covered porch adds plenty of outdoor space to this already impressive home. Built-in cabinets flank the fireplace in the grand room; a fireplace also warms the hearth room. The gourmet kitchen includes an island counter, large walk-in pantry, and serving bar. A secluded home office, with a separate entrance nearby, provides a quiet work place. A front parlor provides even more room for entertaining or relaxing. The master suite dominates the second floor, offering a spacious sitting area with an elegant tray ceiling, a dressing area, and a luxurious bath with two walk-in closets, double vanities, and a raised garden tub. The second floor is also home to an enormous exercise room and three additional bedrooms.

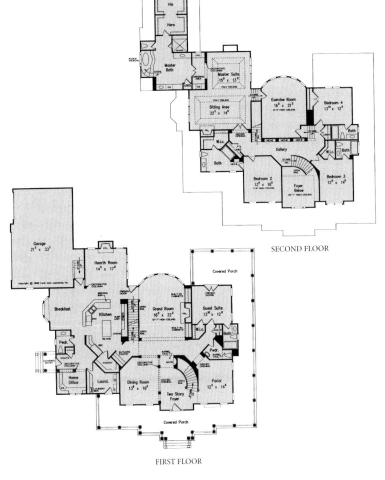

SECOND FLOOR

FIRST FLOOR

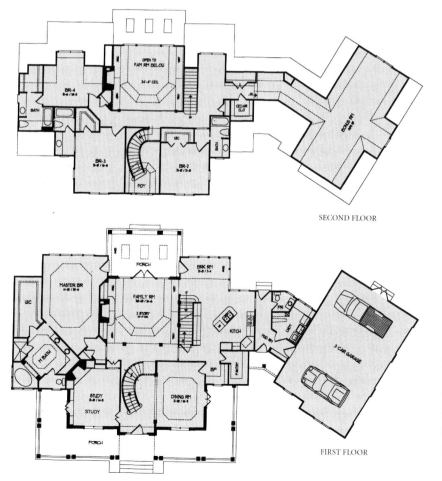

SECOND FLOOR

FIRST FLOOR

plan # HPK0800123

Style: Southern Colonial
First Floor: 2,524 sq. ft.
Second Floor: 1,050 sq. ft.
Total: 3,574 sq. ft.
Bonus Space: 520 sq. ft.
Bedrooms: 4
Bathrooms: 4½
Width: 107' - 7"
Depth: 58' - 7"
Foundation: Basement

SEARCH ONLINE @ EPLANS.COM

The wraparound porch extends
a warm welcome to family and friends alike.
Inside, the study and dining room flank the
foyer. Straight ahead, the family room,
enhanced by a tray ceiling, is warmed by a fireplace on the left wall. The master bedroom,
family room, and breakfast area each enjoy a
private entrance to the rear porch. Upstairs
houses three additional family bedrooms, three
full baths, and a bonus room. A three-car
garage completes this plan.

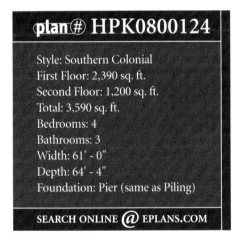

plan# HPK0800124

Style: Southern Colonial
First Floor: 2,390 sq. ft.
Second Floor: 1,200 sq. ft.
Total: 3,590 sq. ft.
Bedrooms: 4
Bathrooms: 3
Width: 61' - 0"
Depth: 64' - 4"
Foundation: Pier (same as Piling)

SEARCH ONLINE @ EPLANS.COM

This luxurious waterfront design

sings of southern island influences. A front covered porch opens to a foyer, flanked by a study and dining room. The living room, warmed by a fireplace and safe from off-season ocean breezes, overlooks the rear covered porch. The island kitchen extends into a breakfast room. Beyond the covered porch, the wood deck is also accessed privately from the master suite. This suite includes a private whirlpool bath and huge walk-in closet. A guest suite is located on the first floor, while two additional bedrooms and a multimedia room are located on the second level.

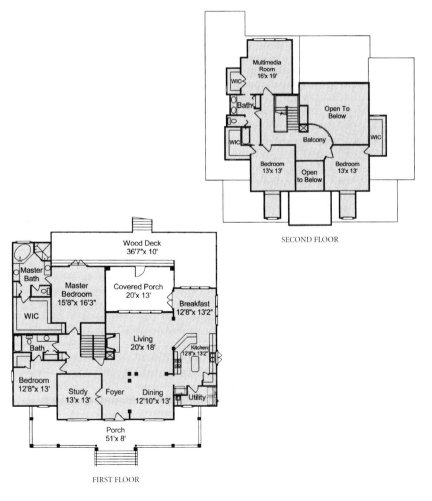

SECOND FLOOR

FIRST FLOOR

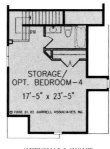

STORAGE/
OPT. BEDROOM-4
17'-5" x 23'-5"

© 2000, 01, 02 GARRELL ASSOCIATES, INC.

OPTIONAL LAYOUT

COVERED
PORCH

KEEPING ROOM
15'-6" x 16'-4"

COVERED PORCH

SITTING
11'-11" x 6'-11"

BREAKFAST
12'-4" x 10'-4"

GRAND ROOM
16'-2" x 18'-4"

MASTER BEDROOM
19'-5" x 14'-0"

PAN.

KITCHEN
15'-5" x 14'-6"

BEDROOM #2
12'-2" x 11'-9"

GALLERY

M. BATH

P.R.

DINING ROOM
15'-0" x 12'-0"

FOYER

STUDY
11'-4" x 13'-7"

W.I.C.

BEDROOM #3
12'-2" x 12'-2"

HERS   HIS

LAUNDRY

COVERED PORCH

OPT.
DN

FIRST FLOOR

TWO CAR GARAGE
22'-3" x 23'-5"

© 2000, 01, 02 GARRELL ASSOCIATES, INC.

plan # HPK0800125

Style: Southern Colonial
Square Footage: 2,807
Bedrooms: 3
Bathrooms: 2½
Width: 68' - 0"
Depth: 83' - 9"
Foundation: Basement

SEARCH ONLINE @ EPLANS.COM

Three covered porches highlight this country design. Once inside, the foyer offers three options: straight ahead leads to the grand room, to the left lies the kitchen and bedrooms, and to the right houses the study and the master suite. The large country kitchen, breakfast nook, and adjoining keeping room are ideal for family interaction. Two family bedrooms share a full bath with private vanities. The master suite boasts a sitting area, and a roomy bath with a dual-sink vanity, garden tub, private toilet, separate shower, and His and Hers walk-in closets. Upstairs, flex space provides a storage option or a fourth bedroom.

plan # HPK0800126

Style: Southern Colonial
Square Footage: 1,373
Bedrooms: 3
Bathrooms: 2
Width: 50' - 4"
Depth: 45' - 0"
Foundation: Basement, Crawlspace

SEARCH ONLINE @ EPLANS.COM

A steep gable roofline punctuated with dormer windows and a columned front porch give a traditional welcome to this family home. A vaulted ceiling tops the family and dining rooms, which are nicely accented with a fireplace and bright windows. An amenity-filled kitchen opens to the breakfast room. The master suite has a refined tray ceiling and a vaulted bath. Two family bedrooms, a laundry center, and a full bath—with private access from Bedroom 3—complete this stylish plan.

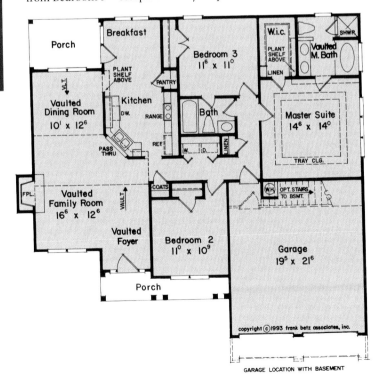

The paired double-end chimneys, reminiscent of the Georgian style of architecture, set this design apart from the rest. The covered entry opens to the columned foyer with the dining room on the left and the living room on the right, each enjoying the warmth and charm of a fireplace. Beyond the grand staircase, the family room delights with a third fireplace and a window wall that opens to the terrace. The expansive kitchen and breakfast area sit on the far left; the master suite is secluded on the the right with its pampering private bath. The second floor holds three additional bedrooms (including a second master bedroom), three full baths, a computer room, and the future recreation room.

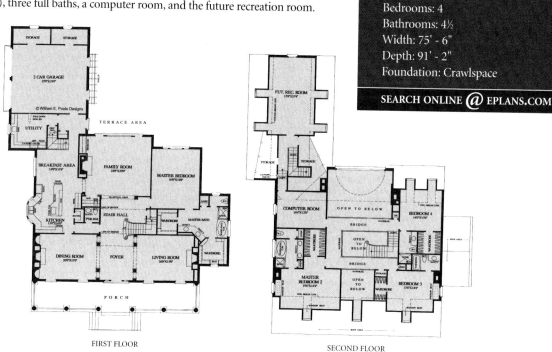

FIRST FLOOR

SECOND FLOOR

ORDER BLUEPRINTS 24 HOURS, 7 DAYS A WEEK, AT 1-800-521-6797

plan⊕ HPK0800128

Style: Country Cottage
First Floor: 1,981 sq. ft.
Second Floor: 291 sq. ft.
Total: 2,272 sq. ft.
Bonus Space: 412 sq. ft.
Bedrooms: 4
Bathrooms: 3½
Width: 58' - 0"
Depth: 53' - 0"
Foundation: Crawlspace

SEARCH ONLINE @ EPLANS.COM

With three dormers and a welcoming front door accented by sidelights and a sunburst, this country cottage is sure to please. The dining room, immediately to the right from the foyer, is defined by decorative columns. In the great room, a volume ceiling heightens the space and showcases a fireplace and built-in bookshelves. The kitchen has plenty of work space and flows into the bayed breakfast nook. A considerate split-bedroom design places the plush master suite to the far left and two family bedrooms to the far right. A fourth bedroom and future space upstairs allow room to grow.

FIRST FLOOR

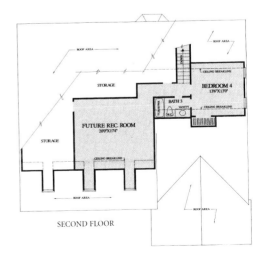

SECOND FLOOR

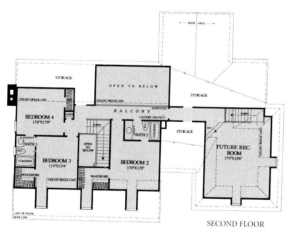

SECOND FLOOR

FIRST FLOOR

plan# HPK0800129

Style: Southern Colonial
First Floor: 1,927 sq. ft.
Second Floor: 879 sq. ft.
Total: 2,806 sq. ft.
Bonus Space: 459 sq. ft.
Bedrooms: 4
Bathrooms: 3½
Width: 71' - 0"
Depth: 53' - 0"
Foundation: Crawlspace

SEARCH ONLINE @ EPLANS.COM

This charming Southern planta-
tion home packs quite a punch in 2,800 square
feet! The elegant foyer is flanked by the formal
dining room and the living room. To the rear,
the family room enjoys a fireplace and expansive view of the outdoors. An archway leads to
the breakfast area and on to the island kitchen.
The luxurious master suite is tucked away for
privacy behind the two-car garage. Three additional bedrooms rest on the second floor where
they share two full baths. Space above the
garage is available for future development.

plan # HPK0800130

Style: Southern Colonial
First Floor: 1,704 sq. ft.
Second Floor: 734 sq. ft.
Total: 2,438 sq. ft.
Bonus Space: 479 sq. ft.
Bedrooms: 3
Bathrooms: 3½
Width: 50' - 0"
Depth: 82' - 6"
Foundation: Crawlspace

SEARCH ONLINE @ EPLANS.COM

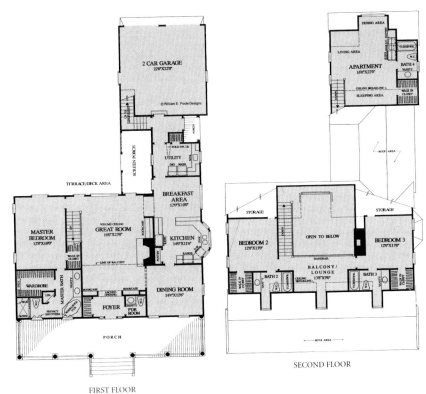

FIRST FLOOR

SECOND FLOOR

Elegant country—that's one way to describe this attractive three-bedroom home. Inside, comfort is evidently the theme, with the formal dining room flowing into the U-shaped kitchen and casual dining taking place in the sunny breakfast area. The spacious, vaulted great room offers a fireplace and built-ins. The first-floor master suite is complete with a walk-in closet, a whirlpool tub, and a separate shower. Upstairs, the sleeping quarters include two family bedrooms with private baths and walk-in closets.

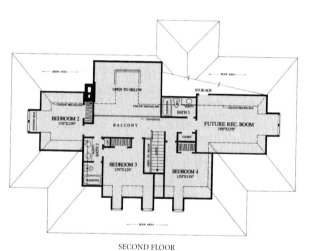

SECOND FLOOR

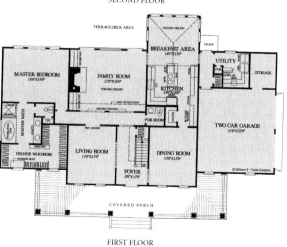

FIRST FLOOR

plan# HPK0800131

Style: Southern Colonial
First Floor: 2,142 sq. ft.
Second Floor: 960 sq. ft.
Total: 3,102 sq. ft.
Bonus Space: 327 sq. ft.
Bedrooms: 4
Bathrooms: 3½
Width: 75' - 8"
Depth: 53' - 0"
Foundation: Crawlspace

SEARCH ONLINE @ EPLANS.COM

Imagine driving up to this cottage beauty at the end of a long week. The long wraparound porch, hipped rooflines, and shuttered windows will transport you. Inside, the foyer is flanked by a living room on the left and a formal dining room on the right. Across the gallery hall, the hearth-warmed family room will surely become the hub of the home. To the right, the spacious kitchen boasts a worktop island counter, ample pantry space, and a breakfast area. A short hallway opens to the utility room and the two-car garage. The master suite takes up the entire left wing of the home, enjoying an elegant private bath and a walk-in closet that goes on and on. Upstairs, three more bedrooms reside, sharing two full baths. Expandable future space awaits on the right.

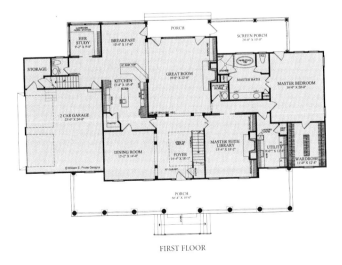

plan# HPK0800132

Style: Southern Colonial
First Floor: 2,891 sq. ft.
Second Floor: 1,336 sq. ft.
Total: 4,227 sq. ft.
Bonus Space: 380 sq. ft.
Bedrooms: 4
Bathrooms: 3½ + ½
Width: 90' - 8"
Depth: 56' - 4"
Foundation: Crawlspace, Basement

SEARCH ONLINE @ EPLANS.COM

This Southern coastal cottage radiates charm and elegance. Step inside from the covered porch and discover a floor plan with practicality and architectural interest. The foyer has a raised ceiling and is partially open to above. The library and great room offer fireplaces and built-in shelves; the great room also provides rear-porch access. The kitchen, featuring an island with a separate sink, is adjacent to the breakfast room and a study with a built-in desk. On the far right, the master bedroom will amaze, with a sumptuous bath and enormous walk-in closet. Three upstairs bedrooms share a loft and recreation room. Convenient storage opportunities make organization easy.

SECOND FLOOR

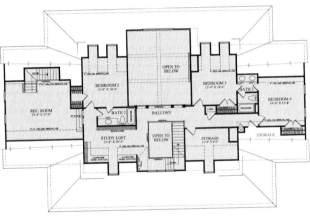

FIRST FLOOR

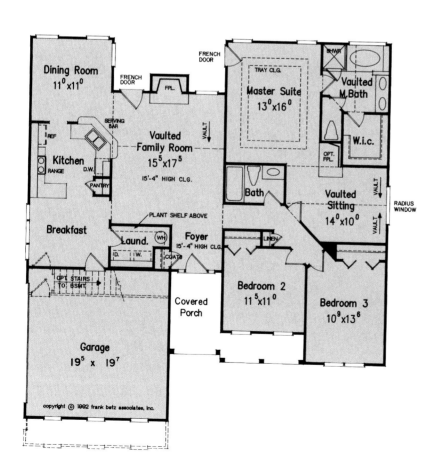

Dining Room
11⁰x11⁰

Kitchen

Breakfast

Laund.

Garage
19⁵ x 19⁷

copyright © 1992 frank betz associates, inc.

FRENCH DOOR

SERVING BAR

Vaulted
Family Room
15⁵x17⁵

15'-4" HIGH CLG.

PLANT SHELF ABOVE

Foyer
15'-4" HIGH CLG.

OPT. STAIRS
TO BSMT.

Covered
Porch

FRENCH DOOR

FPL

Master Suite
13⁰x16⁰

TRAY CLG.

VAULT

Bath

Bedroom 2
11⁵x11⁰

Vaulted
M. Bath

W.i.c.

OPT. FPL

Vaulted
Sitting
14⁰x10⁰

VAULT

LINEN

RADIUS WINDOW

Bedroom 3
10⁹x13⁶

plan # HPK0800133

Style: Southern Colonial
Square Footage: 1,671
Bedrooms: 3
Bathrooms: 2
Width: 50' - 0"
Depth: 51' - 0"
Foundation: Slab,
Crawlspace, Basement

SEARCH ONLINE @ EPLANS.COM

Asymmetrical gables, a columned porch, and an abundance of windows brighten the exterior of this compact home. An efficient kitchen boasts a pantry and a serving bar that it shares with the formal dining room and the vaulted family room. A sunny breakfast room and nearby laundry room complete the living zone. Be sure to notice extras such as the focal-point fireplace in the family room and a plant shelf in the laundry room. The sumptuous master suite offers a door to the backyard, a vaulted sitting area, and a pampering bath. Two family bedrooms share a hall bath.

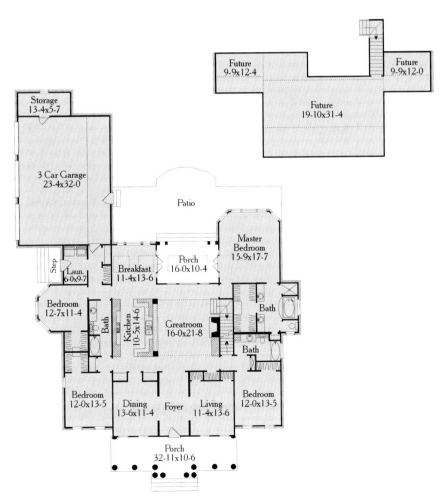

plan# HPK0800134

Style: Southern Colonial
Square Footage: 2,863
Bedrooms: 4
Bathrooms: 3
Width: 73' - 8"
Depth: 97' - 9"
Foundation: Basement,
Crawlspace, Slab

SEARCH ONLINE @ EPLANS.COM

A pedimented front porch gives this Southern Colonial home a classic appeal. Inside, the living and dining rooms face each other across the foyer. At the center of the plan is the great room with a fireplace and built-ins. Skylights flood the covered porch and breakfast room with light. Escape the busy world in the master suite with a bay window and a luxurious bath. Two secondary bedrooms are placed on the opposite side of the home—one with a beautiful bay window—and a third is at the front right.

A covered porch with a recessed entry is crowned with the addition of a front gable. A symmetrical plan of living areas places the living and dining rooms to either side of the foyer, with the family room directly ahead. A graceful arched opening and a fireplace flanked by windows are complemented by extra-high ceilings in the foyer and family room. An efficiently designed kitchen features an abundance of counter and cabinet space along with a serving bar to the breakfast nook. The master suite is separated from the two family bedrooms for privacy.

plan# HPK0800135

Style: Southern Colonial
Square Footage: 1,856
Bedrooms: 3
Bathrooms: 2
Width: 59' - 0"
Depth: 54' - 6"
Foundation: Slab, Basement, Crawlspace

SEARCH ONLINE @ EPLANS.COM

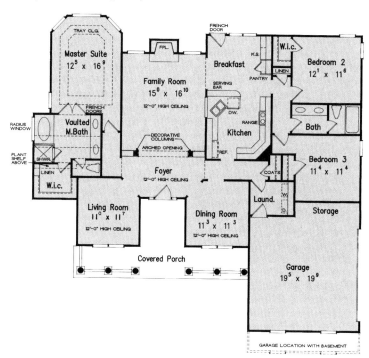

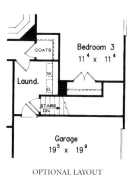

OPTIONAL LAYOUT

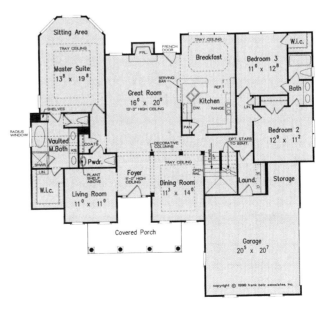

plan # HPK0800136

Style: Country Cottage
Square Footage: 2,072
Bonus Space: 372 sq. ft.
Bedrooms: 3
Bathrooms: 2½
Width: 61' - 0"
Depth: 58' - 6"
Foundation: Crawlspace, Basement

SEARCH ONLINE @ EPLANS.COM

Horizontal siding and a columned porch indicate country flavor in this fine three-bedroom home. Inside, the foyer is flanked by a formal living room and dining room; directly ahead, the great room—with a fireplace—opens to the breakfast room and kitchen. Two family bedrooms share a full bath, and the private master suite is full of amenities. Upstairs, an optional fourth bedroom provides plenty of future expansion opportunities.

© 2003, Garrell Associates, Inc.

Gracious living starts with a balanced and appealing facade. Enjoy the open pediment above the covered porch and the shutters framing the front windows. A formal dining room offers just the right amount of space for get-togethers. The family room does double duty for guests and casual time. An adjoining sunroom is a perfect spot to close the evening or start the day. Breakfast will be bright with natural light from the bay just off the kitchen. Two bedrooms, split from the master, are secluded to the right of the plan and share a full bath. A large walk-in closet and private bath outfit the master suite.

plan# HPK0800137

Style: Southern Colonial
Square Footage: 1,985
Bonus Space: 191 sq. ft.
Bedrooms: 3
Bathrooms: 2
Width: 54' - 0"
Depth: 54' - 0"
Foundation: Slab

SEARCH ONLINE @ EPLANS.COM

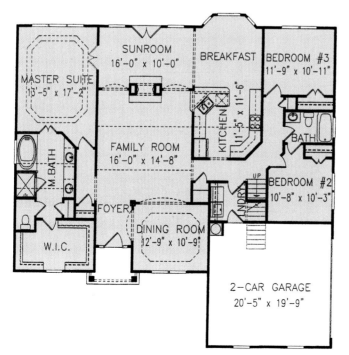

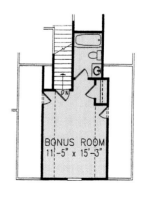

© Copyright 2004, Garrell Associates, Inc.

plan ⊕ HPK0800138

Style: Southern Colonial
First Floor: 3,179 sq. ft.
Second Floor: 1,265 sq. ft.
Total: 4,444 sq. ft.
Bonus Space: 626 sq. ft.
Bedrooms: 4
Bathrooms: 4½
Width: 81' - 8"
Depth: 75' - 10"
Foundation: Basement

SEARCH ONLINE @ EPLANS.COM

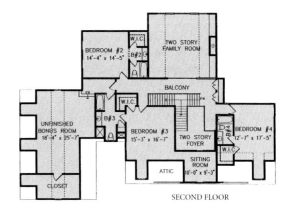

SECOND FLOOR

Three dormers and a columned

covered porch welcome visitors to this country dream home. The right side of the bottom floor is dominated by the master bedroom, which includes an optional private entry to the adjacent study. Fireplaces in the family room and keeping room warm the adjoining kitchen and breakfast nook. The rear screened porch and terrace is conveniently accessed from this area. Upstairs, an unfinished bonus room offers space for future expansion. Three family bedrooms, each with a full bath, complete the second floor.

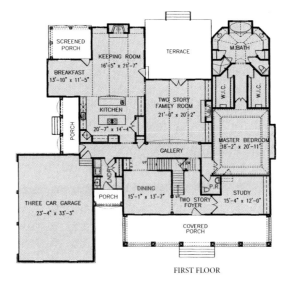

FIRST FLOOR

SECOND FLOOR

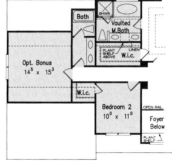

OPTIONAL LAYOUT

FIRST FLOOR

plan# HPK0800139

Style: Southern Colonial
First Floor: 1,103 sq. ft.
Second Floor: 759 sq. ft.
Total: 1,862 sq. ft.
Bonus Space: 342 sq. ft.
Bedrooms: 4
Bathrooms: 3
Width: 50' - 4"
Depth: 35' - 0"
Foundation: Crawlspace,
Basement, Slab

SEARCH ONLINE @ EPLANS.COM

This charming country home speaks well of an American vernacular style, with classic clapboard siding, shutters, and sash windows—all dressed up for 21st-Century living. A flex room on the first floor can be a study, playroom, or fourth bedroom. The casual living space enjoys a fireplace, wide views of the rear property, and a French door to the outside. Upstairs, the master suite features a vaulted bath with separate shower, dual vanity, and walk-in closet with linen storage.

plan # HPK0800140

Style: Southern Colonial
First Floor: 1,237 sq. ft.
Second Floor: 1,098 sq. ft.
Total: 2,335 sq. ft.
Bedrooms: 3
Bathrooms: 2½
Width: 29' - 4"
Depth: 73' - 0"
Foundation: Slab

SEARCH ONLINE @ EPLANS.COM

The curb appeal of this home can be found in the dazzling details: a bay window, twin sconces illuminating a columned porch, a pretty portico, and classic shutters. The foyer opens to the formal living and dining rooms, subtly defined by a central fireplace. The gourmet kitchen overlooks a spacious family/breakfast area, which leads outdoors. The second floor includes a lavish master suite with a spa-style tub and a private covered balcony. The secondary sleeping area is connected by a gallery hall and a stair landing.

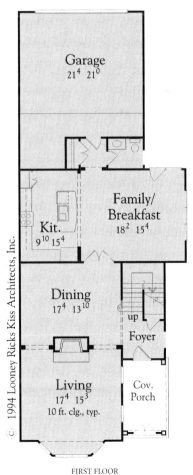

FIRST FLOOR

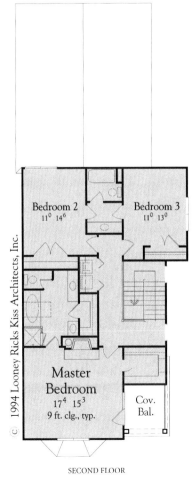

SECOND FLOOR

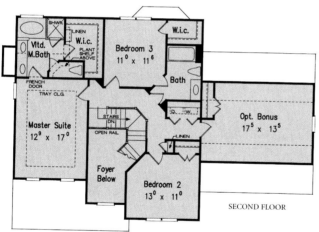

SHWR | LINEN
Vltd. | W.i.c.
M.Bath | PLANT SHELF ABOVE
FRENCH DOOR
TRAY CLG.

Bedroom 3
11⁰ x 11⁶

W.i.c.

Bath

Master Suite
12⁹ x 17⁰

STAIRS DN
OPEN RAIL

LINEN

Opt. Bonus
17⁵ x 13⁵

Foyer Below

Bedroom 2
13⁰ x 11⁰

SECOND FLOOR

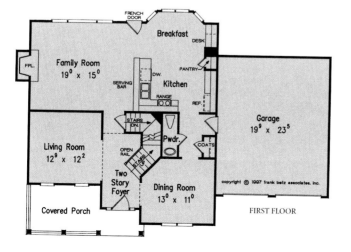

FRENCH DOOR

Breakfast

DESK

Family Room
19⁰ x 15⁰

FPL

SERVING BAR

DW

Kitchen

PANTRY

RANGE

REF.

Garage
19⁹ x 23⁵

STAIRS DN
OPEN RAIL

Pwdr.

COATS

Living Room
12⁹ x 12²

Two Story Foyer

Dining Room
13⁰ x 11⁰

copyright © 1997 frank betz associates, inc.

Covered Porch

FIRST FLOOR

plan# HPK0800141

Style: Southern Colonial
First Floor: 1,071 sq. ft.
Second Floor: 924 sq. ft.
Total: 1,995 sq. ft.
Bonus Space: 280 sq. ft.
Bedrooms: 3
Bathrooms: 2½
Width: 55' - 10"
Depth: 38' - 6"
Foundation: Crawlspace, Basement, Slab

SEARCH ONLINE @ EPLANS.COM

Move-up buyers can enjoy all the luxuries of this two-story home highlighted by an angled staircase separating the dining room from casual living areas. A private powder room is tucked away behind the dining room—convenient for formal dinner parties. A bay window and built-in desk in the breakfast area are just a few of the plan's amenities. The sleeping zone occupies the second floor—away from everyday activities—and includes a master suite and two secondary bedrooms.

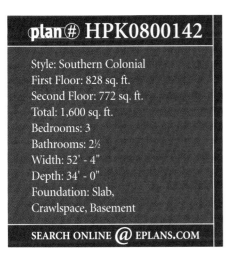

plan# HPK0800142

Style: Southern Colonial
First Floor: 828 sq. ft.
Second Floor: 772 sq. ft.
Total: 1,600 sq. ft.
Bedrooms: 3
Bathrooms: 2½
Width: 52' - 4"
Depth: 34' - 0"
Foundation: Slab,
Crawlspace, Basement

SEARCH ONLINE @ EPLANS.COM

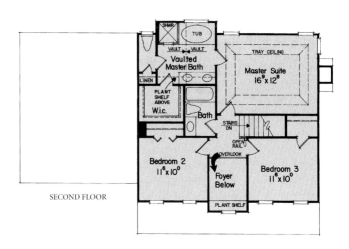

SECOND FLOOR

Traditional farmhouse symmetry is apparent throughout this family plan. The formal dining and living rooms split off of the foyer; each has two multipane windows facing forward. The comfortable family room has a fireplace at the far end and a French door to the rear yard. Most notable is the spacious feeling that comes from the family room being open to the breakfast room and the kitchen. Upstairs, the master suite is detailed with a tray ceiling and a vaulted master bath. Two family bedrooms and a hall bath complete this plan.

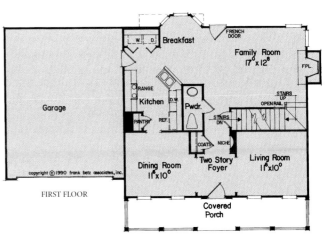

FIRST FLOOR

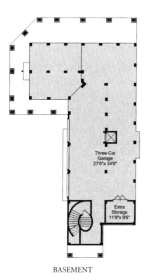

BASEMENT

FIRST FLOOR

SECOND FLOOR

plan# HPK0800143

Style: Southern Colonial
First Floor: 2,578 sq. ft.
Second Floor: 1,277 sq. ft.
Total: 3,855 sq. ft.
Bedrooms: 4
Bathrooms: 4
Width: 53' - 6"
Depth: 97' - 0"
Foundation: Pier (same as Piling)

SEARCH ONLINE @ EPLANS.COM

plan# HPK0800144

Style: Southern Colonial
First Floor: 2,236 sq. ft.
Second Floor: 1,208 sq. ft.
Total: 3,444 sq. ft.
Bedrooms: 4
Bathrooms: 4
Width: 42' - 6"
Depth: 71' - 4"
Foundation: Pier (same as Piling)

SEARCH ONLINE @ EPLANS.COM

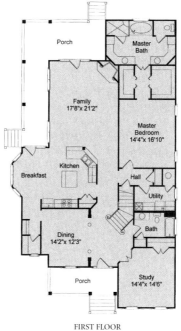

FIRST FLOOR

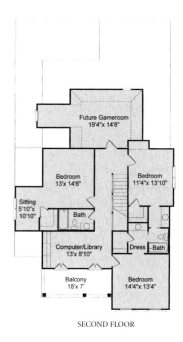

SECOND FLOOR

plan# HPK0800145

Style: Southern Colonial
First Floor: 1,901 sq. ft.
Second Floor: 1,874 sq. ft.
Total: 3,775 sq. ft.
Bedrooms: 4
Bathrooms: 3½
Width: 50' - 0"
Depth: 70' - 0"
Foundation: Pier (same as Piling)

SEARCH ONLINE @ EPLANS.COM

This elegant Charleston townhouse

is enhanced by Southern grace and three levels of charming livability. Covered porches offer outdoor living space at every level. The first floor offers a living room warmed by a fireplace, an island kitchen serving a bayed nook, and a formal dining room. A first-floor guest bedroom is located at the front of the plan, along with a laundry and powder room. The second level offers a sumptuous master suite boasting a private balcony, a master bath, and enormous walk-in closet. Two other bedrooms sharing a Jack-and-Jill bath are also on this level. The basement level includes a three-car garage and game room warmed by a fireplace.

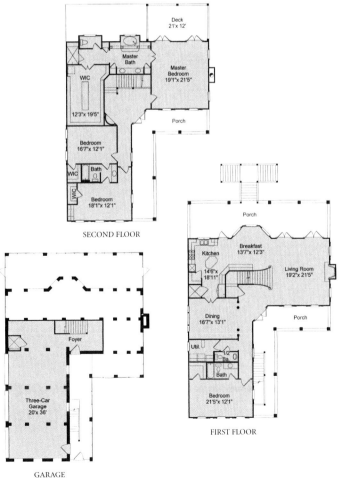

SECOND FLOOR

GARAGE

FIRST FLOOR

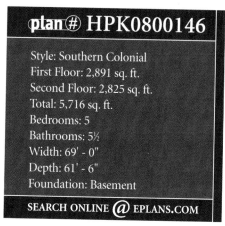

SECOND FLOOR

SITTING AREA

MASTER SUITE
17'-5" x 22'-10"

M. BATH

TWO STORY
VERANDA

BEDROOM 5
15'-5" x 17'-2"

ENTRY ROTUNDA

WARDROBE

READING ROOM
10'-6" x 19'-3"

W.I.C. BATH

BATH

STAIR HALL

LINEN

BATH

W.I.C.

LINEN

W.I.C.

BEDROOM 3
14'-3" x 17'-3"

STAIR HALL
SITTING AREA
10'-2" x 17'-3"

BEDROOM 4
14'-5" x 14'-3"

PORCH

FIRST FLOOR

OPEN PORCH

FAMILY ROOM
15'-6" x 16'-8"

BREAKFAST
15'-6" x 15'-11"

TWO STORY
VERANDA

MINI MASTER
BEDROOM
15'-5" x 18'-11"

HOME OFFICE

GALLERY

KITCHEN
17'-9" x 16'-11"

LIVING ROOM
15'-0" x 16'-0"

M. BATH

21'-3" x 19'-7"

LAUNDRY

GALLERY

W.I.C.

THREE CAR
GARAGE
23'-9" x 11'-3"

PWDR

DINING ROOM
14'-3" x 17'-3"

FOYER

LIBRARY
14'-5" x 13'-10"

PORCH

plan# HPK0800146

Style: Southern Colonial
First Floor: 2,891 sq. ft.
Second Floor: 2,825 sq. ft.
Total: 5,716 sq. ft.
Bedrooms: 5
Bathrooms: 5½
Width: 69' - 0"
Depth: 61' - 6"
Foundation: Basement

SEARCH ONLINE @ EPLANS.COM

Columned porches on both levels create a stately appearance for this Colonial beauty. Inside, a mini-master bedroom can serve as a luxurious guest suite. The open design of the kitchen and family room coupled with the adjacent two-story veranda make for easy family interaction. Upstairs, the master suite offers a massive, amenity-filled retreat, complete with a sitting area, huge wardrobe, and roomy master bath. Three additional family bedrooms each boast a full bath. A sitting area and a reading room complete this floor.

ORDER BLUEPRINTS 24 HOURS, 7 DAYS A WEEK, AT 1-800-521-6797

© Copyright 2004, Garrell Associates, Inc.

plan# HPK0800147

Style: Southern Colonial
First Floor: 2,642 sq. ft.
Second Floor: 2,479 sq. ft.
Total: 5,121 sq. ft.
Bonus Space: 339 sq. ft.
Bedrooms: 4
Bathrooms: 5½
Width: 76' - 0"
Depth: 51' - 0"
Foundation: Basement

SEARCH ONLINE @ EPLANS.COM

A wealth of windows lends abundant natural light to this classic Colonial design. Once inside, the kitchen immediately impresses with a U-shaped serving bar accessible to the grand room and the butler's pantry. The breakfast area/sunroom offers a bayed view of the backyard and access to a rear deck. The kitchen area is flanked by the grand room on the right and the keeping room on the left. A home office and a library/guest suite complete the first floor. Upstairs, the immense master suite, complete with a sitting room, His and Hers walk-in closets, a roomy bath, and an optional exercise room, is the main attraction. Three additional family bedrooms with full baths, an optional TV room, and a convenient second floor laundry room complete this plan.

FIRST FLOOR

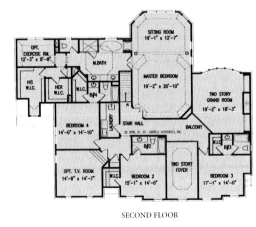

SECOND FLOOR

The exterior is just a taste of the luxury that awaits inside. This plan features two master bedrooms, one upstairs and one downstairs—take your pick. The first floor master is conveniently located next to the library and accesses a rear two-story covered porch. The second story master boasts a sitting room and access to a rear balcony. Three additional family bedrooms, each with a full bath, complete the second level.

plan# HPK0800148

Style: Southern Colonial
First Floor: 3,156 sq. ft.
Second Floor: 2,557 sq. ft.
Total: 5,713 sq. ft.
Bedrooms: 5
Bathrooms: 5½
Width: 71' - 0"
Depth: 58' - 8"
Foundation: Basement

SEARCH ONLINE @ EPLANS.COM

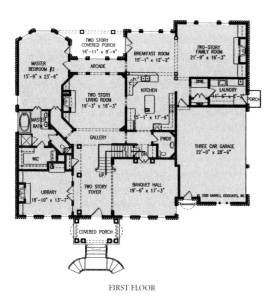

FIRST FLOOR

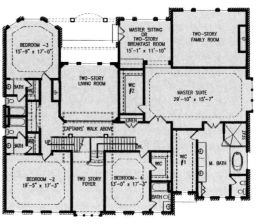

SECOND FLOOR

ORDER BLUEPRINTS 24 HOURS, 7 DAYS A WEEK, AT 1-800-521-6797

© Copyright 2004, Garrell Associates, Inc.

plan# HPK0800149

Style: Southern Colonial
First Floor: 2,902 sq. ft.
Second Floor: 2,791 sq. ft.
Total: 5,693 sq. ft.
Bedrooms: 5
Bathrooms: 5½
Width: 72' - 10"
Depth: 67' - 6"
Foundation: Basement

SEARCH ONLINE @ EPLANS.COM

A classic Colonial exterior and contemporary amenity-filled interior combine to create an extraordinary home. The large grand room opens to the keeping room and kitchen making for an ideal space for entertaining and family interaction. The first floor is warmed nicely by four fireplaces in the library, the grand room, the keeping room, and the banquet hall. Upstairs, the master bedroom, flanked by a private entrance to a covered porch, features a spacious master bath complete with huge woman's and man's wardrobes. Three additional family bedrooms with full baths and a conveniently located second floor laundry room complete this level. A fifth bedroom on the first floor serves as a guest or in-law suite.

FIRST FLOOR

SECOND FLOOR

© Copyright 2004, Garrell Associates, Inc.

This classic Colonial home beautifully embodies old and new. Inside, the large grand room is the heart of the home. With access to a rear covered porch and deck, it welcomes outdoor living. Upstairs, the master suite, enhanced by a tray ceiling, features a sitting area, dual-sink vanity, garden tub, private toilet, separate shower, and walk-in closet. Three family bedrooms, two full baths, and a study loft complete this floor.

plan# HPK0800150

Style: Southern Colonial
First Floor: 1,649 sq. ft.
Second Floor: 1,604 sq. ft.
Total: 3,253 sq. ft.
Bedrooms: 4
Bathrooms: 3½
Width: 69' - 6"
Depth: 53' - 8"
Foundation: Basement, Slab

SEARCH ONLINE @ EPLANS.COM

OPTIONAL DECK

DECK

COVERED PORCH

BREAKFAST
11'-1" x 15'-5"

FLEX SPACE
THIRD CAR GARAGE
15'-3" x 21'-6"

TWO STORY
REAR
FOYER

KIT
16'-0"

GRAND ROOM
24'-8" x 15'-10"

PAN.

LAUNDRY

P.R.

GALLERY

TWO CAR GARAGE
20'-5" x 23'-7"

STUDY
11'-9" x 11'-9"

FOYER

DINING ROOM
11'-10" x 13'-8"

PORCH

FIRST FLOOR

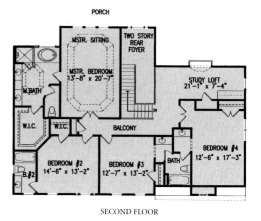

PORCH

MSTR. SITTING

TWO STORY
REAR
FOYER

MSTR. BEDROOM
13'-8" x 20'-7"

M.BATH

STUDY LOFT
21'-1" x 7'-4"

W.I.C.

W.I.C.

BALCONY

BEDROOM #2
14'-6" x 13'-2"

BEDROOM #3
12'-7" x 13'-2"

BATH

BEDROOM #4
12'-6" x 17'-3"

B.#2

SECOND FLOOR

ORDER BLUEPRINTS 24 HOURS, 7 DAYS A WEEK, AT 1-800-521-6797

GREEK REVIVAL

As the Colonial period gave way to the Romantic, the newly formed United States were growing at a fantastic pace and celebrating their independence. That spirit of independence led to an appreciation of another great democratic society, and as new homes sprang up across the country, they began to embrace Greek architecture.

There are a number of interpretations of the Greek Revival style, including different roofs—front-gabled, side-gabled, hipped—and porch configurations. Certain identifying characteristics are consistent, however, beginning with prominent cornice lines at the base of the roof. A wide band of trim—both beneath the cornice and on porches—add decorative touches.

Detailed front doors can create gorgeous entryways in Greek Revival homes. Windows typically surround the door on three sides, with woodworking details adorning the perimeter of the door as well.

The front porch, supported by prominent columns, was a prominent feature on Greek Revivals. This style marked the first widespread introduction of the front porch in the United States. Like other Colonial homes, regional interpretations provided variations on Greek Revival houses. The full-height, full-width front porch, for example, was prominent in the South, but rarely found north of the Carolinas. ■

The windows surrounding the front door of Design HPK0800155 (page 160) help make it a perfect example of Greek Revival design.

SECOND FLOOR

FIRST FLOOR

© William E. Poole Designs

plan# HPK0800151

Style: Greek Revival
First Floor: 3,749 sq. ft.
Second Floor: 1,631 sq. ft.
Total: 5,380 sq. ft.
Bonus Space: 1,171 sq. ft.
Bedrooms: 4
Bathrooms: 4½ + ½
Width: 92' - 4"
Depth: 112' - 0"
Foundation: Crawlspace, Basement

SEARCH ONLINE @ EPLANS.COM

This stately manor brings to mind the grandeur of a fading age. The pedimented, columned porch commands awe and acts as centerpiece to the perfectly symmetrical facade. Inside, formality reigns at the front of the plan, with an elegant dining room and formal living room flanking the large foyer. Ahead, past the staircase, find the gallery hall, which opens through double columns to the more casual family room. Here, a warming hearth and outdoor access will be enjoyed by family and guests. Another set of double columns on the left introduces the breakfast area and island kitchen. To the rear of these rooms, convenience is provided by a half-bath, mudroom, and utility area. A truly pampering master suite resides on the opposite side of the plan. Upstairs, three bedrooms each have a private bath. An exercise room, rec room, and office space complete the second floor.

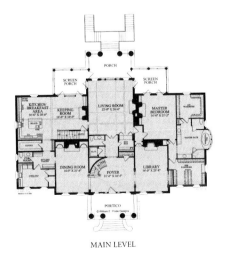

plan # HPK0800152

Style: Greek Revival
Main Level: 4,572 sq. ft.
Second Level: 3,152 sq. ft.
Lower Level: 2,918 sq. ft.
Total: 10,642 sq. ft.
Bedrooms: 6
Bathrooms: 7½ + ½
Width: 97' - 2"
Depth: 81' - 2"
Foundation: Basement

SEARCH ONLINE @ EPLANS.COM

Come home to true Southern glamour in this stunning Greek Revival. Imposing columns enclose a double porch, creating a dramatic entrance. The foyer showcases a spiral staircase and opens to a formal dining room on the left and a library on the right—both warmed by fireplaces. The family will love spending quality time in the huge hearth-warmed living room, which opens to a rear triple porch. On the left of the plan, the island kitchen is expanded by a breakfast area and keeping room. Elegance abounds in the right wing, where the master suite takes center stage. The second floor is home to four spacious bedrooms—one with a fireplace—two baths, and a playroom. A balcony that opens to the second-level porch also overlooks the foyer below. The lower level of this home is its own little world, with a pub, rec room, efficiency kitchen, hobby, and exercise rooms, and another full bath and bedroom.

LOWER LEVEL

MAIN LEVEL

UPPER LEVEL

The entry to this classic home is framed with a sweeping double staircase and four large columns topped with a pediment. The two-story foyer is flanked by spacious living and dining rooms. The two-story family room, which has a central fireplace, opens to the study and a solarium. A spacious U-shaped kitchen features a central island cooktop. An additional staircase off the breakfast room offers convenient access to the second floor. The impressive master suite features backyard access and a bath fit for royalty. Four bedrooms upstairs enjoy large proportions.

plan # HPK0800153

Style: Greek Revival
First Floor: 3,902 sq. ft.
Second Floor: 2,159 sq. ft.
Total: 6,061 sq. ft.
Bedrooms: 5
Bathrooms: 3½
Width: 85' - 3"
Depth: 74' - 0"
Foundation: Walkout Basement

SEARCH ONLINE @ EPLANS.COM

FIRST FLOOR

SECOND FLOOR

plan # HPK0800154

Style: Greek Revival
First Floor: 3,505 sq. ft.
Second Floor: 1,302 sq. ft.
Total: 4,807 sq. ft.
Bedrooms: 5
Bathrooms: 4½
Width: 89' - 4"
Depth: 87' - 0"
Foundation: Slab

SEARCH ONLINE @ EPLANS.COM

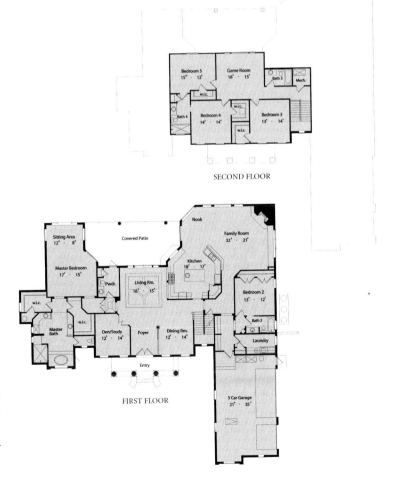

This majestic Early American mansion presents a sturdy, formal outside appearance; inside, it is especially well suited for a large family that likes big informal get-togethers. The huge family room, with a corner fireplace that merges with a dining nook and adjoins the country-style kitchen, will surely be the center of activity. Five bedrooms are placed throughout the home's two levels, including a glorious master suite with all the comforts you've ever dreamed about. A game room joins three bedrooms upstairs. For formal socializing, the dining area and living room are easily entered from the foyer, which guests reach through the impressive pillars of the covered entry. A den, or make it a study, is also located near the front. To the rear is a covered patio, perfect for meals alfresco.

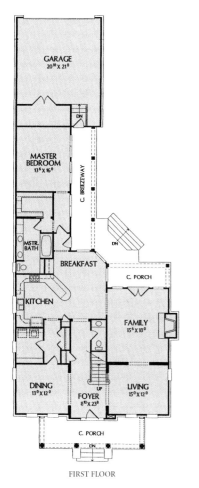

FIRST FLOOR

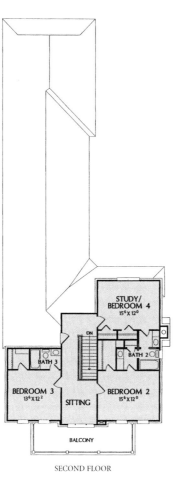

SECOND FLOOR

plan# HPK0800155

Style: Greek Revival
First Floor: 1,886 sq. ft.
Second Floor: 1,016 sq. ft.
Total: 2,902 sq. ft.
Bedrooms: 3
Bathrooms: 3½
Width: 39' - 7"
Depth: 107' - 5"
Foundation: Crawlspace

SEARCH ONLINE @ EPLANS.COM

Doric columns, a simple balustrade,

and an elliptical fanlight transom play in perfect harmony on this distinctive Village or Edge home. The foyer announces a gracious interior, starting with heart-stoppingly beautiful formal rooms. The dining room employs a butler's pantry to accommodate planned events. A relaxed but well-organized kitchen overlooks the casual living space, which has a fireplace. Lovely French doors lead outside to a covered porch and breezeway—a perfect beginning for a stroll around the neighborhood. The master suite provides a deluxe bath designed to please the homeowner.

© William E. Poole Designs, Inc.

plan # HPK0800156

Style: Greek Revival
First Floor: 2,473 sq. ft.
Second Floor: 1,447 sq. ft.
Total: 3,920 sq. ft.
Bonus Space: 428 sq. ft.
Bedrooms: 4
Bathrooms: 3½
Width: 68' - 8"
Depth: 80' - 0"
Foundation: Crawlspace, Basement

SEARCH ONLINE @ EPLANS.COM

The grand appearance of this Greek Revival home is timeless. Inside, the family room is enhanced by a central fireplace, a built-in bookcase, and access to a rear porch. The adjacent master suite boasts His and Hers wardrobes, a whirlpool tub, a dual-sink vanity, and a private toilet and shower. The right side of the first floor features a side porch that leads to the mud room. The island kitchen will be a family favorite with wrap-around counter space, a built-in desk, a walk-in pantry, and a sunporch that doubles as a breakfast area. The second floor houses a second master suite, or possible guest suite, complete with all of the amenities of the first floor master. Two additional family bedrooms share a full bath. A future rec room above the garage completes this plan.

FIRST FLOOR

SECOND FLOOR

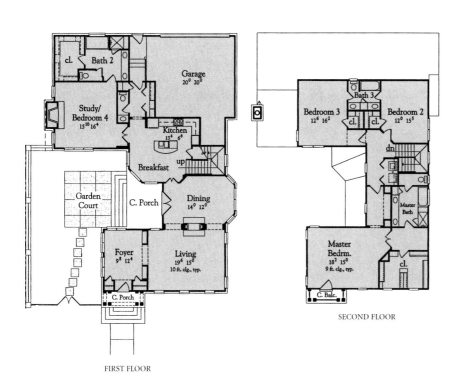

FIRST FLOOR

SECOND FLOOR

plan# HPK0800157

Style: Greek Revival
First Floor: 1,681 sq. ft.
Second Floor: 1,342 sq. ft.
Total: 3,023 sq. ft.
Bedrooms: 3
Bathrooms: 3½
Width: 46' - 9"
Depth: 68' - 0"
Foundation: Crawlspace

SEARCH ONLINE @ EPLANS.COM

A finely crafted porch and covered balcony complement classical elements, such as a portico and triple symmetrical dormers, on this stately yet charming townhome. The entry leads to a foyer that's brightened by three sets of windows. A through-fireplace connects a crowd-size living room and a formal dining room that leads to a side porch and courtyard. The first-floor bedroom has a fireplace and easily converts to a study. A rear-loading garage keeps the car out of public view but handy for out-of-town errands.

plan# HPK0800158

Style: Greek Revival
First Floor: 4,209 sq. ft.
Second Floor: 2,097 sq. ft.
Total: 6,306 sq. ft.
Bedrooms: 4
Bathrooms: 4½
Width: 122' - 0"
Depth: 98' - 0"
Foundation: Basement

SEARCH ONLINE @ EPLANS.COM

Details, details—they make a significant difference in this posh estate home. The exterior reverberates with classic touches fit for any English Country home. The interior is lavish in its use of space and decoration. The opposing library and grand salon capture an elegant era in entertaining—the dining room just beyond complements both. The keeping room, however, is surrounded in glass and connects to the breakfast room and island kitchen. In a completely separate wing, the master suite has its own sitting room, two cedar closets, His and Hers dressing areas, and His and Hers closets. This suite accesses the pool/spa area, which is highlighted by a trellised arbor. Upstairs bedrooms include one large enough to be used as a second master suite.

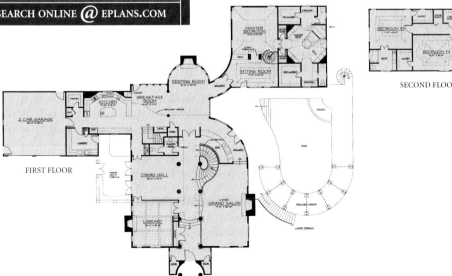

FIRST FLOOR

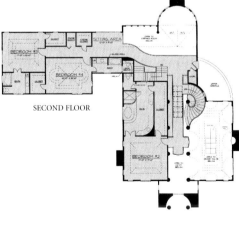

SECOND FLOOR

SECOND FLOOR

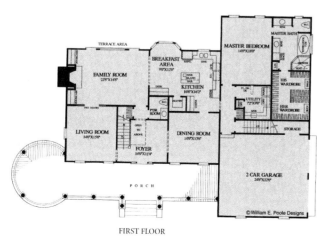

FIRST FLOOR

plan# HPK0800159

Style: Greek Revival
First Floor: 2,099 sq. ft.
Second Floor: 1,260 sq. ft.
Total: 3,359 sq. ft.
Bonus Space: 494 sq. ft.
Bedrooms: 4
Bathrooms: 3½
Width: 68' - 4"
Depth: 54' - 0"
Foundation: Crawlspace

SEARCH ONLINE @ EPLANS.COM

This colonial home gets a Victorian treatment with an expansive covered porch complete with a gazebo-like terminus. Inside, the impressive foyer is flanked by the living room and the formal dining room. The spacious island kitchen is ideally situated between the dining room and the sunny breakfast area. Completing the living area, the family room enjoys a fireplace, built-ins, and a generous view. The lavish master suite resides on the far right with a private bath and a huge walk-in closet. A second master suite is found on the upper level, along with two additional bedrooms which share a full bath.

plan# HPK0800160

Style: Greek Revival
First Floor: 1,807 sq. ft.
Second Floor: 1,970 sq. ft.
Total: 3,777 sq. ft.
Bedrooms: 4
Bathrooms: 3½
Width: 57' - 4"
Depth: 53' - 6"
Foundation: Basement

SEARCH ONLINE @ EPLANS.COM

For sheer magnificence, this chateau-style mansion is unbeatable. Guests will be enchanted, both by the pillared entry and the inside splendor. The two-story grand room, with an extended-hearth fireplace, is well designed for unforgettable soiree's. A front dining room and living room (or make it a library) radiate a gracious welcome. The kitchen can easily serve gourmet dinners and informal family meals. It opens to an exquisite breakfast bay with five windows and to a keeping room with a fireplace. All four bedrooms are situated upstairs, and the posh master suite enjoys His and Hers walk-in closets and vanities. The laundry is conveniently located on this floor.

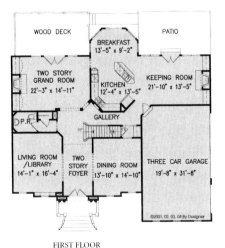

FIRST FLOOR

SECOND FLOOR

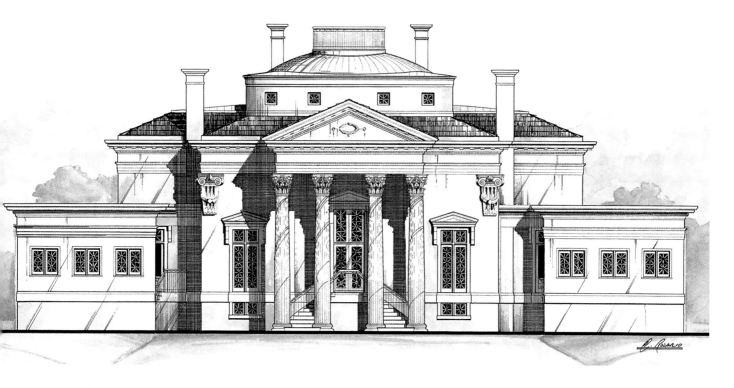

This is a grand design——there is no denying it. Symmetrical, ornate, historical, and complex, it speaks to those with the discretion to investigate a very particular kind of estate home. Interior spaces are adorned with distinctive details. The entry and gallery focus on circular stairs with double access to the second-floor landing. Each of the living areas has a unique and decorative ceiling treatment. Even the master bath is enhanced beyond the ordinary. Aspects to appreciate: a formal library, two walk-in pantries, a master bedroom vestibule, double garages, a private master bedroom porch, an elevator, and a gigantic storage area on the second floor.

plan# HPK0800161

Style: Greek Revival
First Floor: 3,340 sq. ft.
Second Floor: 1,540 sq. ft.
Third Floor: 850 sq. ft.
Total: 5,730 sq. ft.
Bedrooms: 4
Bathrooms: 4½
Width: 106' - 0"
Depth: 82' - 0"
Foundation: Basement

SEARCH ONLINE @ EPLANS.COM

THIRD FLOOR

BASEMENT

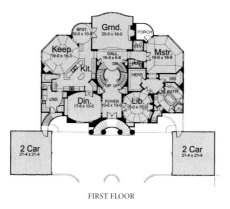

FIRST FLOOR

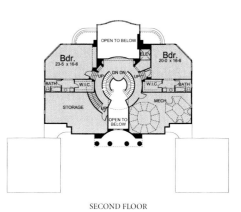

SECOND FLOOR

plan# HPK0800162

Style: Greek Revival
First Floor: 1,332 sq. ft.
Second Floor: 1,331 sq. ft.
Total: 2,663 sq. ft.
Bedrooms: 4
Bathrooms: 3½
Width: 48' - 0"
Depth: 42' - 0"
Foundation: Basement

SEARCH ONLINE @ EPLANS.COM

Hints of Greek Revivalism blend beautifully with Early American style for a handsome home with world-wide appeal. The entry is gracefully lit by a second-story arched window and leads guests into a bayed living room. The great room is ready to host any occasion, with a corner fireplace and built-in entertainment center. The kitchen has a central island and easily serves the breakfast nook and dining area. Upstairs, three bedrooms line the right side of the plan, and the master suite is on the left. Here, vaulted ceilings and walk-in closets are lovely luxuries, but the real standout is the bath, with a whirlpool tub and a see-through fireplace shared with the bedroom.

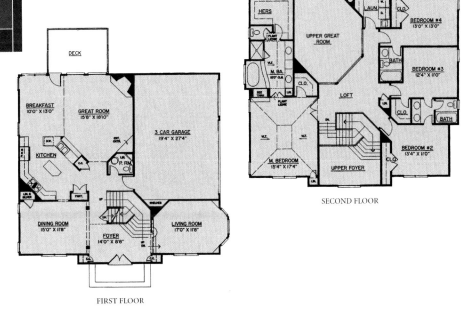

SECOND FLOOR

FIRST FLOOR

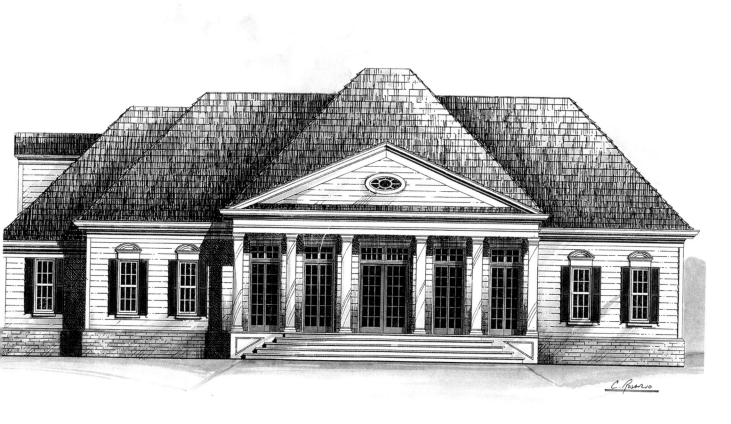

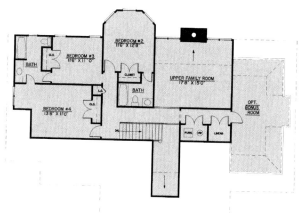

SECOND FLOOR

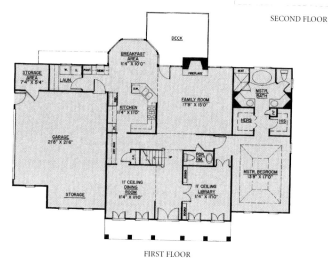

FIRST FLOOR

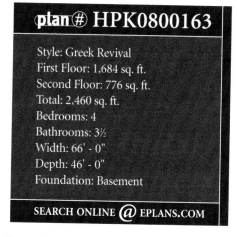

plan# HPK0800163

Style: Greek Revival
First Floor: 1,684 sq. ft.
Second Floor: 776 sq. ft.
Total: 2,460 sq. ft.
Bedrooms: 4
Bathrooms: 3½
Width: 66' - 0"
Depth: 46' - 0"
Foundation: Basement

SEARCH ONLINE @ EPLANS.COM

The stately pillars that highlight the facade of this Greek Revival home invite all visitors to enter into the spacious two-story foyer, beyond which lie a treasure of amenities. Both the dining room and the library, which flank the foyer, have twin sets of French doors that open onto the front porch. The huge family room with a cozy fireplace flows smoothly into the kitchen and breakfast bay. The entire right wing encompasses the master suite, truly a testimony to fine living. Upstairs, three bedrooms share two baths. Additional second-level space can be developed for expansion.

SECOND FLOOR

plan# HPK0800164

Style: Greek Revival
First Floor: 3,509 sq. ft.
Second Floor: 1,564 sq. ft.
Total: 5,073 sq. ft.
Bedrooms: 4
Bathrooms: 4½ + ½
Width: 86' - 6"
Depth: 67' - 3"
Foundation: Walkout Basement

SEARCH ONLINE @ EPLANS.COM

Classic symmetry sets off this graceful exterior, with two sets of double columns framed by tall windows and topped with a detailed pediment. Just off the foyer, the study and dining room present an elegant impression. The gourmet kitchen offers a food-preparation island and a lovely breakfast bay. The central gallery hall connects casual living areas with the master wing. A delightful dressing area with a split vanity and a bay window indulge the lavish master bath. The master bedroom features a bumped-out glass sitting area, a tray ceiling, and a romantic fireplace. Upstairs, three bedroom suites are pampered with private baths.

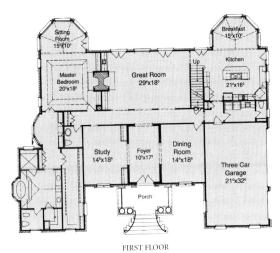

FIRST FLOOR

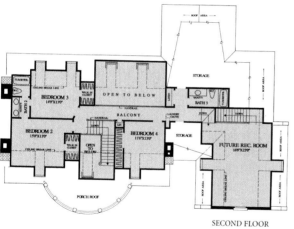

SECOND FLOOR

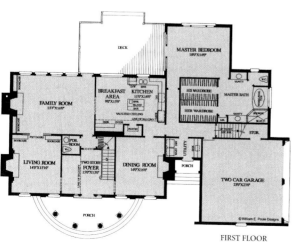

FIRST FLOOR

Sturdy columns on a spacious, welcoming front porch lend a Greek Revival feel to this design, and three dormer windows provide a relaxed country look. The living and dining rooms, each with a fireplace, flank the two-story foyer; the family room also includes a fireplace, as well as built-in shelves and a wall of windows. The L-shaped kitchen, conveniently near the breakfast area, features a work island and a large pantry. Two walk-in closets highlight the lavish master suite, which offers a private bath with a soothing whirlpool tub. Three family bed-rooms—all with dormer alcoves and two with walk-in closets—sit upstairs, along with a future recreation room.

© William E. Poole Designs, Inc.

plan# HPK0800004

Style: Greek Revival
First Floor: 1,688 sq. ft.
Second Floor: 630 sq. ft.
Total: 2,318 sq. ft.
Bonus Space: 506 sq. ft.
Bedrooms: 3
Bathrooms: 3½
Width: 44' - 4"
Depth: 62' - 4"
Foundation: Crawlspace, Basement

SEARCH ONLINE @ EPLANS.COM

This Southern Colonial beauty features three porches: one welcomes visitors to the first floor, the second offers a pleasant retreat from a bedroom upstairs, and the third, a screened porch, sits at the rear of the house, accessed from the great room. A centrally located fireplace in the great room warms the entire area, including the kitchen and the breakfast room. The spacious kitchen is a family favorite with a snack bar and a scenic view of the backyard. The left side of the plan is dominated by the master suite. The master bath boasts a dual sink vanity, a whirlpool tub, a separate shower, a compartmented toilet, and His and Hers walk-in closets. Upstairs, there are two additional family bedrooms, each with a full bath. Future space on the second floor invites the possibility of a fourth bedroom and a recreation room. A two-car garage completes the plan.

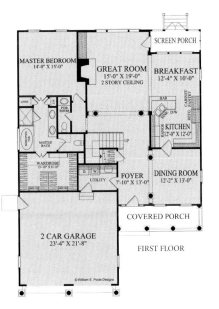

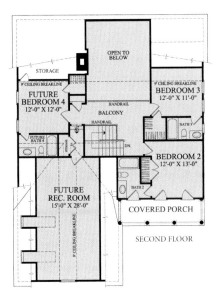

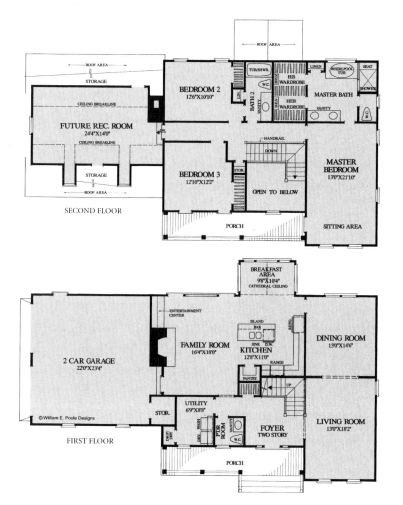

SECOND FLOOR

- ROOF AREA
- STORAGE
- CEILING BREAKLINE
- **FUTURE REC. ROOM** 24'4"X14'0"
- CEILING BREAKLINE
- STORAGE
- ROOF AREA

BEDROOM 2 12'6"X10'10"

ROOF AREA

TUB/SHWR. | HIS WARDROBE | LINEN | WHIRLPOOL TUB | SEAT
BATH 2 | W.C. | HER WARDROBE | **MASTER BATH** | SHOWER
VANITY | VANITY | W.C.

HANDRAIL
DOWN

BEDROOM 3 12'10"X12'2"
STOR.

OPEN TO BELOW

MASTER BEDROOM 13'0"X21'10"

PORCH

SITTING AREA

FIRST FLOOR

2 CAR GARAGE 22'0"X23'4"

© William E. Poole Designs

FAMILY ROOM 16'4"X18'0"

ENTERTAINMENT CENTER

BREAKFAST AREA 9'8"X10'4" CATHEDRAL CEILING

ISLAND
BAR
SINK | D.W.
KITCHEN 12'8"X11'0"
RANGE
PANTRY

REFG.

DINING ROOM 13'0"X14'6"

STOR.

UTILITY 6'9"X8'6"
DRIP/DRY | WASH | PDR ROOM | VANITY | W.C.

UP

FOYER TWO STORY

LIVING ROOM 13'0"X18'2"

PORCH

plan# HPK0800166

Style: Greek Revival
First Floor: 1,291 sq. ft.
Second Floor: 1,087 sq. ft.
Total: 2,378 sq. ft.
Bonus Space: 366 sq. ft.
Bedrooms: 3
Bathrooms: 2½
Width: 65' - 4"
Depth: 40' - 0"
Foundation: Crawlspace

SEARCH ONLINE @ EPLANS.COM

This home exudes Early American elegance. Inside, a central fireplace in the family room conveniently warms the adjacent island kitchen and cathedral-ceilinged breakfast area. A built-in entertainment center is an added bonus to this area. Upstairs, the master suite features a sitting area, a dual-sink vanity, a private toilet, whirlpool tub, separate shower, and His and Hers walk-in closets. Two additional family bedrooms share a full hall bath.

plan# HPK0800167

Style: Greek Revival
First Floor: 1,209 sq. ft.
Second Floor: 1,005 sq. ft.
Total: 2,214 sq. ft.
Bonus Space: 366 sq. ft.
Bedrooms: 3
Bathrooms: 2½
Width: 65' - 4"
Depth: 40' - 4"
Foundation: Crawlspace

SEARCH ONLINE @ EPLANS.COM

SECOND FLOOR

The rebirth of a style—this design salutes the look of Early America. From the porch, step into the two-story foyer, and either venture to the left towards the living room and dining room, or to the right where the family room sits. A central fireplace in the family room warms the island kitchen. The open design allows unrestricted interaction. Upstairs, the master suite boasts a roomy bath with a dual-sink vanity, a whirlpool tub, a private toilet, a separate shower, and His and Hers walk-in closets. Two additional family bedrooms share a full bath. Future expansion space completes this level.

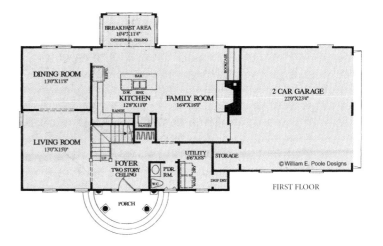

FIRST FLOOR

A handsome porch dressed up with Greek Revival details greets visitors warmly in this Early American home. The foyer opens to the airy and spacious living room and dining room with vaulted ceilings. The secluded master bedroom also sports a vaulted ceiling and is graced with a dressing area, private bath, and walk-in closet. Two decks located at the rear of the plan are accessed via the master bedroom, kitchen, and living room. A full bath serves the two family bedrooms.

plan # HPK0800168

Style: Greek Revival
Square Footage: 1,550
Bedrooms: 3
Bathrooms: 2
Width: 62' - 8"
Depth: 36' - 0"
Foundation: Basement

SEARCH ONLINE @ EPLANS.COM

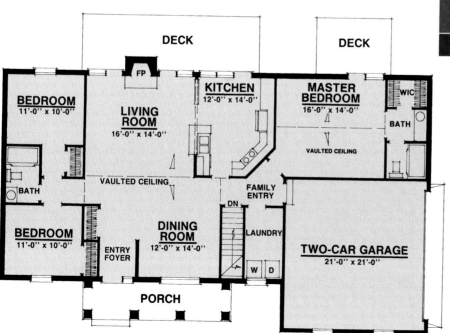

plan# HPK0800169

Style: Greek Revival
Square Footage: 2,394
Bedrooms: 3
Bathrooms: 3
Width: 82' - 6"
Depth: 52' - 8"
Foundation: Crawlspace

SEARCH ONLINE @ EPLANS.COM

A long covered front porch welcomes you to this attractive three-bedroom home. Inside, the foyer opens to the formal living room on the left and also leads back to the comfortable family room. Here, a fireplace, built-ins, and sliding glass doors to the rear deck make it a great place to gather. Two family bedrooms reside on the right side of the home, each with a private bath and a walk-in closet. The homeowner will surely love the master suite, which is full of amenities such as a huge walk-in closet, a whirlpool tub, and separate shower and two vanities.

With an abundance of natural light and amenities, this home is sure to please. The sunporch doubles as a delightful area to enjoy meals with a view. A mud room off the utility room accesses a side porch and serves as a place to hang coats or shed dirty shoes before entering the kitchen or family room. The master bedroom, family room, and living room/library each boast a private fireplace. Upstairs houses three additional bedrooms, two sharing a full bath and one with an attached full bath. Future expansion space completes the second floor. Extra storage space in the garage is an added convenience.

plan# HPK0800170

Style: Greek Revival
First Floor: 2,337 sq. ft.
Second Floor: 1,016 sq. ft.
Total: 3,353 sq. ft.
Bonus Space: 394 sq. ft.
Bedrooms: 4
Bathrooms: 3½
Width: 66' - 2"
Depth: 71' - 2"
Foundation: Crawlspace

SEARCH ONLINE @ EPLANS.COM

Here is a beautiful example of Classical Revival architecture complete with shuttered, jack-arch windows and a column-supported pediment over the entry. Inside, the foyer opens to the living room and leads to the family room at the rear. Here, a panoramic view is complemented by an impressive fireplace framed by built-ins. To the left, the efficient island kitchen is situated between the sunny breakfast nook and the formal dining room. The right side of the plan holds two bedrooms and the lavish master suite.

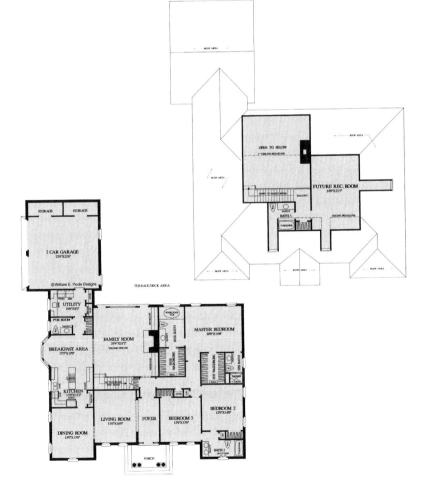

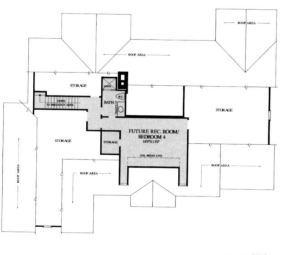

plan# HPK0800172

Style: Greek Revival
Square Footage: 2,639
Bonus Space: 396 sq. ft.
Bedrooms: 3
Bathrooms: 2½
Width: 73' - 8"
Depth: 58' - 6"
Foundation: Crawlspace

SEARCH ONLINE @ EPLANS.COM

Colonial architecture, like this elegant home, lends a classic air to any neighborhood. The interior offers a completely modern arrangement with the dramatic foyer opening to the spectacular living room with its window wall, cathedral ceiling, and stunning fireplace. To the left, the kitchen is central to the more intimate family/sunroom and breakfast area. The formal dining room, to the left of the foyer, completes the living area. The sleeping quarters on the right include two bedrooms and a romantic master suite with its plush private bath.

plan # HPK0800173

Style: Greek Revival
First Floor: 2,449 sq. ft.
Second Floor: 1,094 sq. ft.
Total: 3,543 sq. ft.
Bonus Space: 409 sq. ft.
Bedrooms: 4
Bathrooms: 3½
Width: 89' - 0"
Depth: 53' - 10"
Foundation: Crawlspace

SEARCH ONLINE @ EPLANS.COM

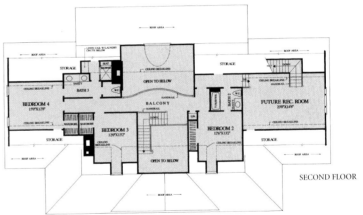

SECOND FLOOR

An impressive front porch coupled with charming twin dormers makes this home a delightful addition to any neighborhood. The sunroom doubles as a delightful area to enjoy meals, a view of the backyard, and gain access to the rear porch. The family room and living room/library each boast a private fireplace. Upstairs houses three additional bedrooms, two sharing a full bath with a dual-sink vanity and one with an attached full bath. Future expansion space and extra storage space complete the second floor.

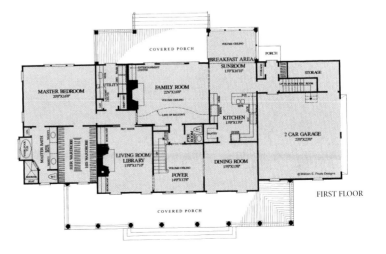

FIRST FLOOR

SECOND FLOOR

FIRST FLOOR

plan # HPK0800174

Style: Greek Revival
First Floor: 2,746 sq. ft.
Second Floor: 992 sq. ft.
Total: 3,738 sq. ft.
Bonus Space: 453 sq. ft.
Bedrooms: 4
Bathrooms: 3½
Width: 80' - 0"
Depth: 58' - 6"
Foundation: Crawlspace

SEARCH ONLINE @ EPLANS.COM

The columned entry of this Colonial home speaks for itself, but the inside actually seals the deal. The cooktop-island kitchen flows easily into the breakfast area and great room. The vaulted-ceiling sunroom accesses a rear covered porch perfect for outdoor entertaining. The master suite enjoys a private entrance to the rear porch, central His and Hers wardrobes, and a spacious bath. Upstairs, three family bedrooms share two full baths. Expansion space makes a future rec room an option. Extra storage space is the garage is an added convenience.

plan# HPK0800175

Style: Greek Revival
Square Footage: 2,987
Bedrooms: 3
Bathrooms: 2½
Width: 74' - 0"
Depth: 62' - 0"
Foundation: Walkout Basement

SEARCH ONLINE @ EPLANS.COM

Reaching back through the centuries for its inspiration, this home reflects the grandeur that was ancient Rome—as it looked to newly independent Americans in the 1700s. The entry portico provides a classic twist: the balustrade that would have marched across the roofline of a typical Revival home trims to form the balcony outside the French doors of the study. Inside, the foyer opens to the study, as well as the formal dining room, then leads to a welcoming great room warmed by a fireplace. The left wing is given over to a private master suite with a bath that offers the ultimate in luxury, including a large walk-in closet. On the right side of the house, two additional bedrooms share a full bath. Separating the sleeping wings is the kitchen, with its nearby keeping/family room.

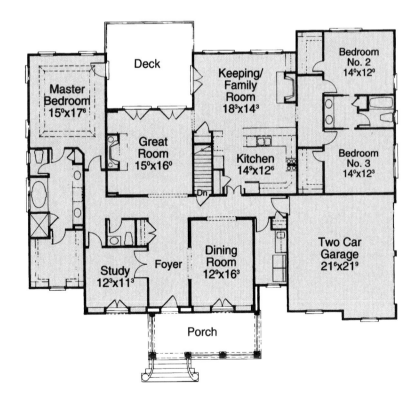

With more than 50 years of experience in the industry and millions of blueprints sold, Hanley Wood is a trusted source of high-quality, high-value pre-drawn home plans.

Using pre-drawn home plans is a **reliable, cost-effective way** to build your dream home, and our vast selection of plans is second-to-none. The nation's finest designers craft these plans that builders know they can trust. Meanwhile, our friendly, knowledgeable customer service representatives can help you every step of the way.

WHAT YOU'LL GET WITH YOUR ORDER

The contents of each designer's blueprint package is unique, but all contain detailed, high-quality working drawings. You can **expect** to find the following standard elements in most sets of plans:

1. FRONT PERSPECTIVE

This artist's sketch of the exterior of the house gives you an idea of how the house will look when built and landscaped.

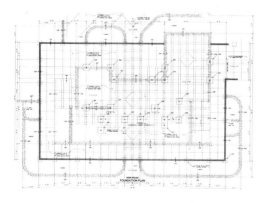

2. FOUNDATION AND BASEMENT PLANS

This sheet shows the foundation layout including concrete walls, footings, pads, posts, beams, and bearing walls, and foundation notes. If the home features a basement, the first-floor framing details may also be included on this plan. If your plan features slab construction rather than a basement, the plan shows footings and details for a monolithic slab. This page, or another in the set, may include a sample plot plan for locating your house on a building site. Additional sheets focus on foundation cross-sections and other details.

3. DETAILED FLOOR PLANS

These plans show the layout of each floor of the house. Rooms and interior spaces are carefully dimensioned, doors and windows located, and keys are given for cross-section details provided elsewhere in the plans.

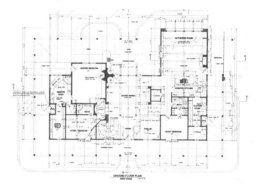

4. HOUSE AND DETAIL CROSS-SECTIONS

Large-scale views show sections or cutaways of the foundation, interior walls, exterior walls, floors, stairways, and roof details. Additional cross-sections may show important changes in floor, ceiling, or roof heights, or the relationship of one level to another. These sections show exactly how the various parts of the house fit together and are extremely valuable during construction. Additional sheets may include enlarged wall, floor, and roof construction details.

5. ROOF AND FLOOR STRUCTURAL SUPPORTS

The roof and floor framing plans provide detail for these crucial elements of your home. Each includes floor joist, ceiling joist, rafter and roof joist size, spacing, direction, span, and specifications. Beam and window headers, along with necessary details for framing connections, stairways, skylights, or dormers are also included.

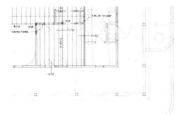

6. ELECTRICAL PLAN

The electrical plan offers a detailed outline of all wiring for your home, with notes for all lighting, outlets, switches, and circuits. A layout is provided for each level, as well as basements, garages, or other structures.

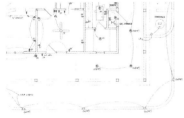

7. EXTERIOR ELEVATIONS

In addition to the front exterior, your blueprint set will include drawings of the rear and sides of your house as well. These drawings give notes on exterior materials and finishes. Particular attention is given to cornice detail, brick and stone accents, or other finish items that make your home unique.

BEFORE YOU CALL

You are making a terrific decision to use a pre-drawn house plan—it is one you can make with confidence, knowing that your blueprints are crafted by national-award-winning certified residential designers and architects, and trusted by builders.

Once you've selected the plan you want—or even if you have questions along the way—our experienced customer service representatives are available 24 hours a day, seven days a week to help you navigate the home-building process. To help them provide you with even better service, please consider the following questions before you call:

■ Have you chosen or purchased your lot?
If so, please review the building setback requirements of your local building authority before you call. You don't need to have a lot before ordering plans, but if you own land already, please have the width and depth dimensions handy when you call.

■ Have you chosen a builder?
Involving your builder in the plan selection and evaluation process may be beneficial. Luckily, builders know they can have confidence with pre-drawn plans because they've been designed for livability, functionality, and typically are builder-proven at successful home sites across the country.

■ Do you need a construction loan?
Construction loans are unique because they involve determining the value of something that is not yet constructed. Several lenders offer convenient contstruction-to-permanent loans. It is important to choose a good lending partner—one who will help guide you through the application and appraisal process. Most will even help you evaluate your contractor to ensure reliability and credit worthiness. Our partnership with IndyMac Bank, a nationwide leader in construction loans, can help you save on your loan, if needed (see the next page for details).

■ How many sets of plans do you need?
Building a home can typically require a number of sets of blueprints—one for yourself, two or three for the builder and subcontractors, two for the local building department, and one or more for your lender. For this reason, we offer 5- and 8-set plan packages, but your best value is the Reproducible Plan Package. Reproducible plans are accompanied by a license to make modifications and typically up to 12 duplicates of the plan so you have enough copies of the plan for everyone involved in the financing and construction of your home.

■ Do you want to make any changes to the plan?
We understand that it is difficult to find blueprints for a home that will meet all of your needs. That is why Hanley Wood is glad to offer plan Customization Services. We will work with you to design the modifications you'd like to see and to adjust your blueprint plans accordingly—anything from changing the foundation; adding square footage, redesigning baths, kitchens, or bedrooms; or most other modifications. This simple, cost-effective service saves you from hiring an outside architect to make alterations. Modifications may only be made to Reproducible Plan Packages that include the license to modify.

■ Do you have to make any changes to meet local building codes?
While all of our plans are drawn to meet national building codes at the time they were created, many areas required that plans be stamped by a local engineer to certify that they meet local building codes. Building codes are updated frequently and can vary by state, county, city, or municipality. Contact your local building inspection department, office of planning and zoning, or department of permits to determine how your local codes will affect your construction project. The best way to assure that you can make changes to your plan, if necessary, is to purchase a Reproducible Plan Package.

■ Has everyone—from family members to contractors—been involved in selecting the plan?
Building a new home is an exciting process, and using pre-drawn plans is a great way to realize your dreams. Make sure that everyone involved has had an opportunity to review the plan you've selected. While Hanley Wood is the only plans provider with an exchange policy, it's best to be sure all parties agree on your selection before you buy.

CALL TOLL-FREE 1-800-521-6797

Source Key
HPK08

CUSTOMIZE YOUR PLAN –
HANLEY WOOD CUSTOMIZATION SERVICES

Creating custom home plans has never been easier and more directly accessible. Using state-of-the-art technology and top-performing architectural expertise, Hanley Wood delivers on a long-standing customer commitment to provide world-class home-plans and customization services. Our valued customers—professional home builders and individual home owners—appreciate the convenience and accessibility of this interactive, consultative service.

With the Hanley Wood Customization Service you can:
■ Save valuable time by avoiding drawn-out and frequently repetitive face-to-face design meetings

■ Communicate design and home-plan changes faster and more efficiently
■ Speed-up project turn-around time
■ Build on a budget without sacrificing quality
■ Transform master home plans to suit your design needs and unique personal style

All of our design options and prices are impressively affordable. A detailed quote is available for a $50 consultation fee. Plan modification is an interactive service. Our skilled team of designers will guide you through the customization process from start to finish making recommendations, offering ideas, and determining the feasibility of your changes. This level of service is offered to ensure the final modified plan meets your expectations. If you use our service the $50 fee will be applied to the cost of the modifications.

You may purchase the customization consultation before or after purchasing a plan. In either case, it is necessary to purchase the Reproducible Plan Package and complete the accompanying license to modify the plan before we can begin customization.

Customization Consultation **$50**

TOOLS TO WORK WITH YOUR BUILDER

Two Reverse Options For Your Convenience – Mirror and Right-Reading Reverse (as available)

Mirror reverse plans simply flip the design 180 degrees—keep in mind, the text will also be flipped. For a minimal fee you can have one or all of your plans shipped mirror reverse, although we recommend having at least one regular set handy. Right-reading reverse plans show the design flipped 180 degrees but the text reads normally. When you choose this option, we ship each set of purchased blueprints in this format.

Mirror Reverse Fee (indicate the number of sets when ordering)   **$55**
Right Reading Reverse Fee (all sets are reversed)   **$175**

A Shopping List Exclusively for Your Home – Materials List

A customized Materials List helps you plan and estimate the cost of your new home, outlining the quantity, type, and size of materials needed to build your house (with the exception of mechanical system items). Included are framing lumber, windows and doors, kitchen and bath cabinetry, rough and finished hardware, and much more.

Materials List. . . . .**$75 each**
Additional Materials Lists (at original time of purchase only)$20 each

Plan Your Home- Building Process – Specification Outline

Work with your builder on this step-by-step chronicle of 166 stages or items crucial to the building process. It provides a comprehensive review of the construction process and helps you choose materials.
Specification Outline . . . .**$10 each**

Get Accurate Cost Estimates for Your Home – Quote One® Cost Reports

The Summary Cost Report, the first element in the Quote One® package, breaks down the cost of your home into various categories based on building materials, labor, and installation, and includes three grades of construction: Budget, Standard, and Custom. Make even more informed decisions about your project with the second element of our package, the Material Cost Report. The material and installation cost is shown for each of more than 1,000 line items provided in the standard-grade Materials List, which is included with this tool. Additional space is included for estimates from contractors and subcontractors, such as for mechanical materials, which are not included in our packages.

Quote One® Summary Cost Report **$35**
Quote One® Detailed Material Cost Report **$140***
*****Detailed material cost report includes the Materials List**

Learn the Basics of Building – Electrical, Pluming, Mechanical, Construction Detail Sheets

If you want to know more about building techniques—and deal more confidently with your subcontractors—we offer four useful detail sheets. These sheets provide non-plan-specific general information, but are excellent tools that will add to your understanding of Plumbing Details, Electrical Details, Construction Details, and Mechanical Details.

Electrical Detail Sheet **$14.95**
Plumbing Detail Sheet **$14.95**
Mechanical Detail Sheet **$14.95**
Construction Detail Sheet **$14.95**
SUPER VALUE SETS:
Buy any 2: $26.95; Buy any 3: $34.95; Buy All 4: $39.95

▲ Best Value

MAKE YOUR HOME TECH-READY – HOME AUTOMATION UPGRADE

Building a new home provides a unique opportunity to wire it with a plan for future needs. A Home Automation-Ready (HA-Ready) home contains the wiring substructure of tomorrow's connected home. It means that every room—from the front porch to the backyard, and from the attic to the basement—is wired for security, lighting, telecommunications, climate control, home computer networking, whole-house audio, home theater, shade control, video surveillance, entry access control, and yes, video gaming electronic solutions.

Along with the conveniences HA-Ready homes provide, they also have a higher resale value. The Consumer Electronics Association (CEA), in conjunction with the Custom Electronic Design and Installation Association (CEDIA), have developed a TechHome™ Rating system that quantifies the value of HA-Ready homes. The rating system is gaining widespread recognition in the real estate industry.

Developed by CEDIA-certified installers, our Home Automation Upgrade package includes everything you need to work with an installer during the construction of your home. It provides a short explanation of the various subsystems, a wiring floor plan for each level of your home, a detailed materials list with estimated costs, and a list of CEDIA-certified installers in your local area.

Home Automation Upgrade **$250**

DESIGN YOUR HOME – INTERIOR AND EXTERIOR FINISHING TOUCHES

Be Your Own Interior Designer! – Home Furniture Planner

Effectively plan the space in your home using our Hands-On Home Furniture Planner. It's fun and easy—no more moving heavy pieces of furniture to see how the room will go together. The kit includes reusable peel-and-stick furniture templates that fit on a 12"x18" laminated layout board—enough space to lay out every room in your house.

Home Furniture Planning Kit **$15.95**

Enjoy the Outdoors! – Deck Plans

Many of our homes have a corresponding deck plan, sold separately, which includes a Deck Plan Frontal Sheet, Deck Framing and Floor Plans, Deck Elevations, and a Deck Materials List. A Standard Deck Details Package, also available, provides all the how-to information necessary for building any deck. Get both the Deck Plan and the Standard Deck Details Package for one low price in our Complete Deck Building Package. See the price tier chart below and call for deck plan availability.

Deck Details (only) **$14.95**
Deck Building Package . . . . **Plan price + $14.95**

Create a Professionally Designed Landscape – Landscape Plans

Many of our homes have a front-yard Landscape Plan that is complementary in design to the house plan. These comprehensive Landscape Blueprint Packages include a Frontal Sheet, Plan View, Regionalized Plant & Materials List, a sheet on Planting and Maintaining Your Landscape, Zone Maps, and a Plant Size and Description Guide. Each set of blueprints is a full 18" x 24" with clear, complete instructions in easy-to-read type. Our Landscape Plans are available with a Plant & Materials List adapted by horticultural experts to eight regions of the country. Please specify your region when ordering your plan—see region map below. Call for more information about landscape plan availability and applicable regions.

LANDSCAPE & DECK PRICE SCHEDULE

PRICE TIERS	1-SET STUDY PACKAGE	5-SET BUILDING PACKAGE	8-SET BUILDING PACKAGE	1-SET REPRODUCIBLE*
P1	$25	$55	$95	$145
P2	$45	$75	$115	$165
P3	$75	$105	$145	$195
P4	$105	$135	$175	$225
P5	$145	$175	$215	$275
P6	$185	$215	$255	$315

PRICES SUBJECT TO CHANGE   * REQUIRES A FAX NUMBER

TERMS & CONDITIONS

OUR EXCHANGE POLICY

HANLEY WOOD EXCLUSIVE!

Hanley Wood is committed to ensuring your satisfaction with your blueprint order, which is why we're the only provider of pre-drawn house plans to offer an exchange policy. With the exception of Reproducible Plan Package orders, we will exchange your entire first order for an equal or greater number of blueprints from our plan collection within 90 days of the original order. The entire content of your original order must be returned before an exchange will be processed. Please call our customer service department at 1-888-690-1116 for your return authorization number and shipping instructions. If the returned blueprints look used, redlined, or copied, we will not honor your exchange. Fees for exchanging your blueprints are as follows: 20% of the amount of the original order, plus the difference in cost if exchanging for a design in a higher price bracket or less the difference in cost if exchanging for a design in a lower price bracket. (Because they can be copied, Reproducible blueprints are not exchangeable or refundable.) Please call for current postage and handling prices. Shipping and handling charges are not refundable.

ARCHITECTURAL AND ENGINEERING SEALS

Some cities and states now require that a licensed architect or engineer review and "seal" a blueprint, or officially approve it, prior to construction. Prior to application for a building permit or the start of actual construction, we strongly advise that you consult your local building official who can tell you if such a review is required.

LOCAL BUILDING CODES AND ZONING REQUIREMENTS

Each plan was designed to meet or exceed the requirements of a nationally recognized model building code in effect at the time and place the plan was drawn. Typically plans designed after the year 2000 conform to the International Residential Building Code (IRC 2000 or 2003). The IRC is comprised of portions of the three major codes below. Plans drawn before 2000 conform to one of the three recognized building codes in effect at the time: Building Officials and Code Administrators (BOCA) International, Inc.; the Southern

Building Code Congress International, (SBCCI) Inc.; the International Conference of Building Officials (ICBO); or the Council of American Building Officials (CABO).

Because of the great differences in geography and climate throughout the United States and Canada, each state, county, and municipality has its own building codes, zone requirements, ordinances, and building regulations. Your plan may need to be modified to comply with local requirements. In addition, you may need to obtain permits or inspections from local governments before and in the course of construction. We authorize the use of the blueprints on the express condition that you consult a local licensed architect or engineer of your choice prior to beginning construction and strictly comply with all local building codes, zoning requirements, and other applicable laws, regulations, ordinances, and requirements. Notice: Plans for homes to be built in Nevada must be redrawn by a Nevada-registered professional. Consult your local building official for more information on this subject.

TERMS AND CONDITIONS

These designs are protected under the terms of United States Copyright Law and may not be copied or reproduced in any way, by any means, unless you have purchased a Reproducible Plan Package and signed the

accompanying license to modify and copy the plan, which clearly indicates your right to modify, copy, or reproduce. We authorize the use of your chosen design as an aid in the construction of ONE (1) single- or multi-family home only. You may not use this design to build a second dwelling or multiple dwellings without purchasing another blueprint or blueprints or paying additional design fees. Multi-use fees vary by designer—please call one of experienced sales representatives for a quote.

DISCLAIMER

The designers we work with have put substantial care and effort into the creation of their blueprints. However, because we cannot provide on-site consultation, supervision, and control over actual construction, and because of the great variance in local building requirements, building practices, and soil, seismic, weather, and other conditions, WE MAKE NO WARRANTY OF ANY KIND, EXPRESS OR IMPLIED, WITH RESPECT TO THE CONTENT OR USE OF THE BLUEPRINTS, INCLUDING BUT NOT LIMITED TO ANY WARRANTY OF MERCHANTABILITY OR OF FITNESS FOR A PARTICULAR PURPOSE. ITEMS, PRICES, TERMS, AND CONDITIONS ARE SUBJECT TO CHANGE WITHOUT NOTICE.

CALL TOLL-FREE 1-866-473-4052 OR VISIT EPLANS.COM

IMPORTANT COPYRIGHT NOTICE

From the Council of Publishing Home Designers

Blueprints for residential construction (or working drawings, as they are often called in the industry) are copyrighted intellectual property, protected under the terms of the United States Copyright Law and, therefore, cannot be copied legally for use in building. The following are some guidelines to help you get what you need to build your home, without violating copyright law:

1. HOME PLANS ARE COPYRIGHTED

Just like books, movies, and songs, home plans receive protection under the federal copyright laws. The copyright laws prevent anyone, other than the copyright owner, from reproducing, modifying, or reusing the plans or design without permission of the copyright owner.

2. DO NOT COPY DESIGNS OR FLOOR PLANS FROM ANY PUBLICATION, ELECTRONIC MEDIA, OR EXISTING HOME

It is illegal to copy, change, or redraw home designs found in a plan book, CDROM or on the Internet. The right to modify plans is one of the exclusive rights of copyright. It is also illegal to copy or redraw a constructed home that is protected by copyright, even if you have never seen the plans for the home. If you find a plan or home that you like, you must purchase a set of plans from an authorized source. The plans may not be lent, given away, or sold by the purchaser.

3. DO NOT USE PLANS TO BUILD MORE THAN ONE HOUSE

The original purchaser of house plans is typically licensed to build a single home from the plans. Building more than one home from the plans without permission is an infringement of the home designer's copyright. The purchase of a multiple-set package of plans is for the construction of a single home only. The purchase of additional sets of plans does not grant the right to construct more than one home.

4. HOUSE PLANS IN THE FORM OF BLUEPRINTS OR BLACKLINES CANNOT BE COPIED OR REPRODUCED

Plans, blueprints, or blacklines, unless they are reproducibles, cannot be copied or reproduced without prior written consent of the copyright owner. Copy shops and blueprinters are prohibited from making copies of these plans without the copyright release letter you receive with reproducible plans.

5. HOUSE PLANS IN THE FORM OF BLUEPRINTS OR BLACKLINES CANNOT BE REDRAWN

Plans cannot be modified or redrawn without first obtaining the copyright owner's permission. With your purchase of plans, you are licensed to make non-structural changes by "red-lining" the purchased plans. If you need to make structural changes or need to redraw the plans for any reason, you must purchase a reproducible set of plans (see topic 6) which includes a license to modify the plans. Blueprints do not come with a license to make structural changes or to redraw the plans. You may not reuse or sell the modified design.

6. REPRODUCIBILE HOME PLANS

Reproducible plans (for example sepias, mylars, CAD files, electronic files, and vellums) come with a license to make modifications to the plans. Once modified, the plans can be taken to a local copy shop or blueprinter to make up to 10 or 12 copies of the plans to use in the construction of a single home. Only one home can be constructed from any single purchased set of reproducible plans either in original form or as modified. The license to modify and copy must be completed and returned before the plan will be shipped.

7. MODIFIED DESIGNS CANNOT BE REUSED

Even if you are licensed to make modifications to a copyrighted design, the modified design is not free from the original designer's copyright. The sale or reuse of the modified design is prohibited. Also, be aware that any modification to plans relieves the original designer from liability for design defects and voids all warranties expressed or implied.

8. WHO IS RESPONSIBLE FOR COPYRIGHT INFRINGEMENT?

Any party who participates in a copyright violation may be responsible including the purchaser, designers, architects, engineers, drafters, homeowners, builders, contractors, sub-contractors, copy shops, blueprinters, developers, and real estate agencies. It does not matter whether or not the individual knows that a violation is being committed. Ignorance of the law is not a valid defense.

9. PLEASE RESPECT HOME DESIGN COPYRIGHTS

In the event of any suspected violation of a copyright, or if there is any uncertainty about the plans purchased, the publisher, architect, designer, or the Council of Publishing Home Designers (www.cphd.org) should be contacted before proceeding. Awards are sometimes offered for information about home design copyright infringement.

10. PENALTIES FOR INFRINGEMENT

Penalties for violating a copyright may be severe. The responsible parties are required to pay actual damages caused by the infringement (which may be substantial), plus any profits made by the infringer commissions to include all profits from the sale of any home built from an infringing design. The copyright law also allows for the recovery of statutory damages, which may be as high as $150,000 for each infringement. Finally, the infringer may be required to pay legal fees which often exceed the damages.

BLUEPRINT PRICE SCHEDULE

PRICE TIERS	1-SET STUDY PACKAGE	5-SET BUILDING PACKAGE	8-SET BUILDING PACKAGE	1-SET REPRODUCIBLE*
A1	$450	$500	$555	$675
A2	$490	$545	$595	$735
A3	$540	$605	$665	$820
A4	$590	$660	$725	$895
C1	$640	$715	$775	$950
C2	$690	$760	$820	$1025
C3	$735	$810	$875	$1100
C4	$785	$860	$925	$1175
L1	$895	$990	$1075	$1335
L2	$970	$1065	$1150	$1455
L3	$1075	$1175	$1270	$1600
L4	$1185	$1295	$1385	$1775
SQ1				.40/SQ. FT.
SQ3				.55/SQ. FT.
SQ5				.80/SQ. FT.

PRICES SUBJECT TO CHANGE

* REQUIRES A FAX NUMBER

PLAN #	PRICE TIER	PAGE	MATERIALS LIST	QUOTE ONE®	DECK	DECK PRICE	LANDSCAPE	LANDSCAPE PRICE	REGIONS
HPK0800001	SQ1	6							
HPK0800002	L3	8							
HPK0800005	SQ1	12							
HPK0800006	SQ1	13							
HPK0800007	C3	14							
HPK0800008	C4	15							
HPK0800009	C2	16	Y	Y					
HPK0800010	C3	17							
HPK0800011	L2	18							
HPK0800012	C2	19							
HPK0800013	L1	20	Y	Y	ODA008	P3	OLA016	P4	1234568
HPK0800014	SQ1	21							
HPK0800015	L2	22							
HPK0800016	L1	23							
HPK0800018	C1	24	Y						
HPK0800017	C1	24							
HPK0800019	C1	25	Y						
HPK0800020	C1	26							
HPK0800021	C2	27							
HPK0800022	L1	28							
HPK0800023	SQ1	29	Y	Y					
HPK0800024	C3	29	Y	Y	ODA007	P3	OLA018	P3	12345678
HPK0800025	C4	30							
HPK0800026	C3	31	Y	Y					
HPK0800027	C2	32							
HPK0800028	C4	33							
HPK0800029	C1	34	Y						
HPK0800030	C2	35							
HPK0800031	SQ1	36	Y	Y					
HPK0800032	A4	37	Y						
HPK0800033	A3	37	Y						

PLAN #	PRICE TIER	PAGE	MATERIALS LIST	QUOTE ONE®	DECK	DECK PRICE	LANDSCAPE	LANDSCAPE PRICE	REGIONS
HPK0800034	A3	38							
HPK0800035	A3	39							
HPK0800036	C2	40							
HPK0800037	A4	41	Y		ODA016	P2	OLA001	P3	123568
HPK0800039	C4	42							
HPK0800038	C2	42							
HPK0800040	C1	43							
HPK0800041	L2	44							
HPK0800042	C4	45							
HPK0800043	C2	46							
HPK0800044	C2	47	Y						
HPK0800045	C4	48							
HPK0800046	SQ1	50	Y	Y					
HPK0800047	L1	51							
HPK0800048	A4	52							
HPK0800049	C1	52							
HPK0800050	C3	53							
HPK0800051	C2	54							
HPK0800052	C3	55							
HPK0800053	C4	56							
HPK0800054	C3	57							
HPK0800055	SQ1	58							
HPK0800056	SQ1	59							
HPK0800057	L1	60	Y	Y	ODA002	P2	OLA015	P4	123568
HPK0800058	L2	61							
HPK0800059	C1	62							
HPK0800060	C3	63							
HPK0800061	L1	64							
HPK0800062	C2	65							
HPK0800063	C4	66							
HPK0800064	L2	67							

PLAN #	PRICE TIER	PAGE	MATERIALS LIST	QUOTE ONE®	DECK	DECK PRICE	LANDSCAPE	LANDSCAPE PRICE	REGIONS
HPK0800065	C1	68							
HPK0800066	C2	69							
HPK0800067	C2	70							
HPK0800068	C3	71							
HPK0800069	SQ1	72	Y	Y					
HPK0800070	C3	73							
HPK0800071	C4	74							
HPK0800072	L1	75							
HPK0800073	L2	75							
HPK0800074	C1	76							
HPK0800075	C3	77							
HPK0800076	C2	78							
HPK0800077	SQ1	79							
HPK0800078	C2	80							
HPK0800079	SQ1	81							
HPK0800080	SQ1	82	Y	Y					
HPK0800081	C2	83	Y	Y					
HPK0800082	C4	84							
HPK0800083	C3	85							
HPK0800084	C1	86	Y						
HPK0800085	C2	88							
HPK0800086	C4	89							
HPK0800087	C4	90							
HPK0800088	C4	91							
HPK0800089	C4	92							
HPK0800090	C1	93							
HPK0800091	C2	94							
HPK0800092	C3	95							
HPK0800093	C1	96							
HPK0800094	C3	97							
HPK0800095	C4	98							
HPK0800096	C3	99							
HPK0800097	C3	100	Y						
HPK0800098	A2	101	Y						
HPK0800099	A4	102							
HPK0800100	A3	103	Y						
HPK0800101	A4	104	Y						
HPK0800102	A4	105	Y						
HPK0800103	C3	106	Y	Y		OLA010	P3	1234568	
HPK0800104	L1	107							
HPK0800105	C3	108							
HPK0800106	C3	109							
HPK0800107	SQ1	110							
HPK0800108	C2	112							
HPK0800109	C3	113							
HPK0800110	SQ1	114							
HPK0800111	C1	115	Y	Y		OLA015	P4	123568	
HPK0800112	C4	116	Y	Y		OLA015	P4	123568	
HPK0800113	A4	117	Y						
HPK0800003	C4	118							
HPK0800114	L2	119							
HPK0800115	SQ1	120							
HPK0800116	SQ1	121							
HPK0800117	SQ1	122							
HPK0800118	L1	123							
HPK0800119	C3	124							
HPK0800120	SQ1	125							
HPK0800121	SQ1	126							
HPK0800122	SQ1	127							
HPK0800123	SQ1	128							
HPK0800124	SQ1	129							
HPK0800125	C1	130							
HPK0800126	A4	131							
HPK0800127	L2	132							
HPK0800128	A4	133							
HPK0800129	C3	134							
HPK0800130	A4	135							
HPK0800131	C2	136							
HPK0800132	L2	137							
HPK0800133	C1	138							
HPK0800134	SQ1	139	Y						
HPK0800135	C1	140							
HPK0800136	C2	141							
HPK0800137	A4	142							
HPK0800138	C4	143							
HPK0800139	C1	144							
HPK0800140	A4	145							
HPK0800141	C1	146							
HPK0800142	C1	147							
HPK0800143	L1	148							
HPK0800144	C4	148							
HPK0800145	L1	149							
HPK0800146	L1	150							
HPK0800147	L1	151							
HPK0800148	L1	152							
HPK0800149	L1	153							
HPK0800150	C2	154							
HPK0800151	SQ3	156							
HPK0800152	SQ1	157							
HPK0800153	SQ1	158							
HPK0800154	C4	159							
HPK0800155	C3	160							
HPK0800156	L1	161							
HPK0800157	C3	162							
HPK0800158	SQ1	163							
HPK0800159	C4	164							
HPK0800160	C3	165							
HPK0800161	L1	166							
HPK0800162	C1	167	Y						
HPK0800163	A4	168							
HPK0800164	L3	169							
HPK0800165	C2	170							
HPK0800004	C2	171							
HPK0800166	C2	172							
HPK0800167	C2	173							
HPK0800168	A3	174							
HPK0800169	C2	175							
HPK0800170	C4	176							
HPK0800171	C3	177							
HPK0800172	C3	178							
HPK0800173	L1	179							
HPK0800174	L1	180							
HPK0800175	C3	181							

Turn Your
Dream Home
Into A *Reality*

ARTS & CRAFTS HOME PLANS
1-931131-26-0

$14.95 (128 PAGES)
This title showcases 85 home plans in the Craftsman, Prairie and Bungalow styles.

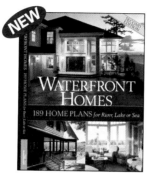

WATERFRONT HOMES
1-931131-28-7

$10.95 (208 PAGES)
A collection of gorgeous homes for those who dream of life on the water's edge—this title features open floor plans with expansive views.

SUN COUNTRY STYLES
1-931131-14-7

$9.95 (192 PAGES)
175 designs from Coastal Cottages to stunning Southwesterns.

Finding the right new home to fit

▶ Your style
▶ Your budget
▶ Your life

...has never been easier.

Our spring collection offers distinctive design coupled with plans to match every wallet. If you are looking to build your new home, look to HomePlanners first.

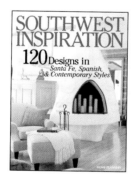

SOUTHWEST INSPIRATION
1-931131-19-8

$14.95 (192 PAGES)
This title features 120 designs in Santa Fe, Spanish and Contemporary styles.

MEDITERRANEAN INSPIRATION
1-931131-09-0

$14.95 (192 PAGES)
Bring home the timeless beauty of the Mediterranean with the gorgeous plans featured in this popular title.

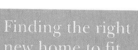

FARMHOUSE & COUNTRY PLANS
1-881955-77-X

$10.95 (320 PAGES)
Farmhouse & Country Plans features 300 fresh designs from classic to modern.

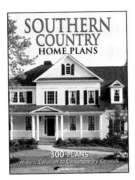

SOUTHERN COUNTRY HOME PLANS
1-931131-06-6

$10.95 (320 PAGES)
Southern Country Home Plans showcases 300 plans from Historic Colonials to Contemporary Coastals.

PROVENCAL INSPIRATION
1-881955-89-3

$14.95 (192 PAGES)
This title features home plans, landscapes and interior plans that evoke the French Country spirit.

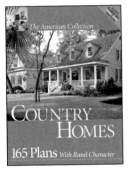

THE AMERICAN COLLECTION: COUNTRY HOMES
1-931131-35-X

$10.95 (192 PAGES)
The American Collection: Country is a must-have if you're looking to build a country home or if you want to bring the relaxed country spirit into your current home.

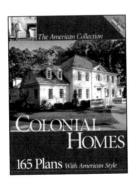

THE AMERICAN COLLECTION: COLONIAL HOMES
1-931131-40-6

$10.95 (192 PAGES)
This beautiful collection features distinctly American home styles—find everything from Colonials, Cape Cod, Georgian, Farmhouse to Saltbox.

PICK UP A COPY TODAY!

Toll-Free:
800.322.6797

Online:
http://books.eplans.com

Hanley Wood HomePlanners provides the largest selection of plans from the nation's top designers and architects. Our special home styles collection offers designs to suit any style.

Colonial homes enjoy a distinct historic charm, without sacrificing modern conveniences. For more details on Design HPK0800025, turn to page 30.